WRITE LIKE A CHAMPION
including 12 Steps to Better Writing

美國老師教你

寫出好英文

Scott Dreyer・廖柏森 合著

眾文圖書股份有限公司

To my primary teachers, my parents: Ken and Jane Dreyer

In the beginning was the Word,
and the Word was with God, and the Word was God.

—*John 1:1*

Acknowledgements

The longer I live, the more I realize that indeed "no man is an island." We are who we are thanks to the people who have invested in our lives. This book is no exception. I am overwhelmed with gratitude when I think of the people who have helped make me the writer and person I am today.

Fang-yu Deborah Dreyer, my wonderful wife and co-traveler, is always encouraging me.

My family has always encouraged communication. For one thing, my parents limited TV usage. Second, mealtimes were natural vocabulary lessons as I heard my older siblings, Larry, Diane, and Mark, using big words they had learned in their high school English classes. Our parents encouraged us to read also.

Our children, Harmony, Sarah, Victor, and David are great sports and also good linguists in their own right.

I was blessed with many excellent teachers, grades 1-12, at the Roanoke County schools I attended. They are too numerous to mention, but a few who stood out and who greatly kindled my interest and skill in the English language were Mrs. Wire (Grade 6), Mrs. Turner (8), Mrs. Bates (9), Ms. Smith (10), and Mr. Brill (AP 12).

Frau Waters, German teacher (9-12), first taught me how to write in a language other than English.

John Holzmann, at the Center for World Mission in Pasadena, California, served as a writing mentor during my summer there in 1988 and introduced me to the genius works of Rudolf Flesch.

Stacy McGuire, friend and gutsy entrepreneur, encouraged me to hurry up and write a book about parenting. "I'd buy it," he urged.

Susan Elkins Groenke, my co-teacher at the Patrick Henry High School Center for the Humanities, taught me much about teaching writing and developing young writers during our one year together, the turn of the Millennium, 1999-2000.

The thousands of students and scores of colleagues I have been blessed to work with over my twenty-year career have helped me become a better writer and communicator.

Dr. John Moore, English professor at William and Mary and instructor at the Southwest Virginia Writing Workshop (Summer 2000) saw poetry in my writing and called it forth.

Dr. Peter Wallenstein, Virginia Tech history professor and accomplished author, has encouraged me as a writer.

In addition, many writing materials have inspired and instructed me over the years, and elements of these works are embedded in this book. *The Art of Readable Writing*, by Rudolf Flesch, is an absolute masterpiece for improving the clarity of one's writing. *Writing Skills Problem Solver*, by Carol H. Behrman, is a useful compilation of writing exercises. *The Word within the Word*, by Michael Clay Thompson, formed the core for the excellent vocabulary program that Susan Elkins Groenke created and that we still use in Patrick Henry High School's Humanities Center. Finally, *Free to Write*, by Roy Peter Clark, is a gem designed to help teachers foster young writers.

This is a small list of acknowledgements, and I send this book out with the hope and prayer that it might inspire others as I have been inspired.

Scott Dreyer

Preface

This book springs from my twenty-plus years of writing, editing, and teaching writing, in both Taiwan and the US. My students have ranged from third graders to Ph.D. candidates in nuclear engineering at National Tsing Hua University. Now, for your convenience, this experience is compiled into one place: this book. My chief goal is to demystify the writing process and help us all become better writers and communicators.

How this book finally came together is a funny story. Shortly before midnight, on Saturday, June 30, 2007, I was both online and on the phone ordering books for the Dreyer Academy Summer Enrichment Writing Class to be held in Hsinchu, Taiwan. One particular writing book I wanted to use was not in stock and could not be delivered until *after* we left the States. Pondering my options for what teaching material to use, an epiphany came to me about 1:00 a.m.: "Write a book yourself!" And how this book came to be bilingual, and into your hands, is yet another great story. I was teaching with this book in Taiwan in its smaller, original form, when Dr. Posen Liao and his wife Liwen Tan approached me about creating an expanded book, with Chinese translation. I am grateful for Liao's co-authorship and guidance. He brings a wealth of knowledge to this project, considering his years of teaching at National Taipei University. His involvement truly makes this book an international product, bringing you the minds of East and West, those who learned English as a foreign language and those who speak it natively.

You can call this book "The ABC's of better writing" because it is organized around three key sections. Part A includes some key elements of better writing and common writing styles (cause and effect, persuasion, etc.). Part B looks at some common grammar and mechanics issues that can be tricky. Part C is the actual "12 Steps" designed to help you write more clearly. Thank you for joining the journey!

And so here it is. Enjoy.

S.G.D.
Roanoke, Virginia
February 2008

序 言

這本書源自我在台灣和美國二十多年寫作、編輯和教授寫作的生涯,我的學生涵括小學三年級生到國立清華大學核子工程的博士候選人。這些教學經驗現在整合成這本書,以饗有心學習寫作的讀者。我撰寫此書主要的目的是希望消弭寫作過程的迷思,並協助更多人成為更佳的寫作者和溝通者。

這本書的成形其實是個有趣的故事,在 2007 年 6 月 30 日週六幾近午夜時分,我同時在網路上和電話上為將在台灣新竹開課的 Dreyer Academy Summer Enrichment 寫作教室訂購教科書,我想採用的一本寫作教科書恰好沒有庫存,而且要到我離開美國後才會供書。當我正傷腦筋要改用哪本教科書之際,近凌晨一點時我突然靈光一閃:「我可以自己寫一本教科書啊!」而現在你手上這本書怎麼會變成中英對照,則是另有一番際遇。後來我在台灣使用這本書的前身,也就是一本篇幅較少的版本在教授寫作時,廖柏森博士與他的夫人譚麗雯女士跟我聯繫,有意擴充原有的版本,並加上中文翻譯。我非常感激廖博士的共同創作和指引,他以在國立台北大學多年的教學經驗和專業知識,對此書的貢獻很大。廖博士的參與使此書真正成為跨國合作的結晶,更是東方以英語為外語和西方以英文為母語兩種心智的融合呈現。

你可以稱這本書為「精進寫作的 ABC」,因為它是以三個主要章節為骨幹。Part A 包含精進寫作的重要元素和常用寫作風格(如因果關係、說服別人等)。Part B 檢視某些容易犯錯的文法和用字的問題。Part C 則是實戰的「12 步驟」,可幫助你的寫作更加清晰流暢。在此先感謝你加入此趟寫作的學習之旅。

現在就請你開卷「悅」讀!

卓文
Roanoke,維吉尼亞州
2008 年 2 月

About the Authors

Scott Dreyer

Scott Dreyer grew up in Roanoke, Virginia, nestled among the beautiful Blue Ridge Mountains. He later attended the College of William and Mary, the second-oldest college in America (established in 1693) and he spent his Junior Year at Westfälische Wilhelms-Universität, in Münster, Germany. He graduated from William and Mary with a B.A. in history and minor in secondary education. He began his teaching career in Henrico County, Virginia, then taught for a decade in Hsinchu, Taiwan, including a five-year stint at the ROC public schools' flagship campus, the National Experimental High School in the Science-based Industrial Park. For two years Dreyer taught English Writing at prestigious National Tsing Hua University, Taiwan's premier engineering school. It was in Taiwan that he also began his editing career: his client list includes China Steel Corporation, the Industrial and Technology Research Institute (ITRI), and various professors from National Tsing Hua University and National Chiao Tung University. It was also during this time that Dreyer earned his M.A. degree in social sciences from Azusa Pacific University. In 1999, Dreyer returned to his hometown of Roanoke, where he teaches at Patrick Henry High School's Center for the Humanities. In 2003, Dreyer was awarded certification by the National Board for Professional Teaching Standards.

This is Dreyer's first book, and he hopes the first of many.

Dreyer lives in Roanoke with his wife Deborah and their four children.

Posen Liao, Ph.D.

Posen Liao earned his Ph.D. degree in Foreign Language Education from the University of Texas at Austin, an M.A. in TESOL from New York University in the United States, and another M.A. in Philosophy from Tunghai University in Taiwan. He is currently an Associate Professor of the Graduate Institute of Translation and Interpretation at National Taiwan Normal University. He previously taught at the TESOL Institute at National Chiao Tung University and at the Department of Foreign Languages and Applied Linguistics at National Taipei University. He has published a variety of research articles and academic books including *The Handbook of Research Paper Writing, Grammar for the Writing of English Research Papers, Collocations for the Writing of English Research Papers, Journalistic English: Reading and Translating, Teaching of English and Translation*, and others. His main research interests are in the areas of academic writing, translation studies, journalistic English, and TESOL.

作者簡介

卓文

卓文成長於維吉尼亞州，位在美麗的藍脊山脈環抱間的 Roanoke。他就讀 William and Mary 學院，是全美第二古老的學院（建於 1693 年），大三時曾留學德國敏斯特的 Westfälische Wilhelms 大學。他在 William and Mary 學院取得文學士學位，主修歷史和副修教育。他首先在維吉尼亞州的 Henrico 郡展開教學生涯，隨後到台灣新竹教書逾十年，其中包括在台灣公立學校中的名校新竹科學園區實驗中學任教五年，以及在工程學術重鎮的清華大學教授兩年英文寫作。他也在台灣開始編修英文論文的工作，客戶包括中鋼公司、工研院、以及清華和交通大學的各系教授。於此同時，卓文於美國 Azusa Pacific University 取得社會科學碩士學位。1999 年返回家鄉 Roanoke 擔任 Patrick Henry 高中人文中心教職，2003 年獲「美國全國教學專業標準委員會」頒發證書。

這是卓文的第一本書，也希望從此能創作更多的書。

卓文現在與妻子潘鳳玉以及四個小孩一起居住在 Roanoke。

廖柏森　博士

美國德州大學奧斯汀分校外語教育哲學博士、紐約大學英語教學碩士、台灣東海大學哲學研究所碩士。現任國立台灣師範大學翻譯研究所副教授。曾任教於國立交通大學英語教學研究所和國立台北大學應用外語學系。著有《英文研究論文寫作——關鍵句指引》、《英文研究論文寫作——文法指引》、《英文研究論文寫作——搭配詞指引》、《新聞英文閱讀與翻譯技巧》、《英語與翻譯教學》等書，並在英語教學和翻譯研究等領域發表多篇中英文學術論文。主要學術興趣為學術寫作、翻譯研究、新聞英文和英語教學。

Contents

Part A

What is Better Writing?
何謂精進寫作？

The "Magical Seven" Elements
魔法七要素

Writing is not like math...maybe that's why I like writing so much. Math is clear cut: for example, 15% of 4,000 is always 600, and even though zero is nothing, try telling that to your math teacher if you answer "6" or "60" to the above question. In contrast, writing is much more fluid, more forgiving. It leaves more room for personal style and quirks.

寫作跟數學不同,這也許就是我熱愛寫作的原因。數學力求明確,例如 4,000 的 15% 永遠都是 600。就算你認為少幾個 0 沒什麼大不了,但你若回答你的數學老師上述題目的答案是 6 或 60,那你就糗大了。相對地,寫作就大有彈性,比較能容許模糊地帶。寫作有很大的空間可以容納個人的風格和癖好。

1 Better Writing is an Extension of You
個人的延伸

So first, better writing is an **extension of you**. When a writer of English sits down with a blank paper (or computer screen) and just 26 letters, he or she tries to create something that has never existed before. You put your own stamp on your writing, just as you have unique fingerprints. Think of what you want to *say*. *Why* are you writing? What do you want to communicate? What do *you personally* have to add to the conversation? If you are only going to parrot what others have said on a particular topic, why write it? Be original; your readers will love you for it. Of course we can learn from other writers' styles and examples, but we should never try to exactly copy another writer. You are unique; let it show in your writing.

所以精進寫作的第一點就是你個人的延伸。英文寫作者面對空白的紙張(或電腦螢幕),嘗試以僅僅 26 個字母創造出前所未有的東西。透過寫作可以留下你個人的印記,如同你獨特的指紋。思考你想說的話,你為何而寫?你想傳達什麼訊息?在對話中可加入哪些個人意見?但如果你只是想複述別人針對某個主題所說過的話,那又何必寫作呢?你一定要有創見,讀者會因你獨特的見解而喜歡你的作品。當然我們也可見賢思齊,學習其他作者的風格和典範,但絕不能完全複製別的作者。你是獨一無二的,讓你的特色表現在寫作上。

2 Better Writing is Clear
敘述清楚

So, while writing is more flexible than math, there *are* rules and guidelines of good practice. Most of all, **writing must be *clear*,** which is point two. If no one can understand you, you have failed in your purpose. And before you can *write* clearly, you must *think* clearly. This is one reason why good writing is so hard, because good *thinking* is so hard. I saw this in an email the other day:

雖然寫作比數學更有彈性，但想要寫好仍需遵循規範和指引。最重要的就是敘述一定要清楚，這是精進寫作的第二點。如果沒人看得懂，那你就白廢工夫了。而要能寫出敘述清楚的文字，你必須先具備清晰的思考。這就是為何好的作品很難得，因為縝密的思考很難得。前幾天我在電子郵件中看到這句話：

- Writing causes thinking.

Likewise, Francis Bacon (1561-1626) once said, "Reading makes a full man [...], but writing makes an exact man."

同樣地，法蘭西斯·培根 (1561-1626) 也曾說過：「閱讀造就完整的人……，但寫作造就的是嚴謹的人。」

So, since writing requires clear thinking and hard work, and since writing in a foreign language is a *big* challenge, no wonder examples of poor written English are everywhere. The other day I saw this on a box of tissues:

因為寫作要求清晰的思考和努力的過程，而用外文寫作又是一大挑戰，這也難怪到處充斥難以入目的英文寫作。前幾天我在面紙盒上看到以下這句話：

- Magic in joy life, free in place, no anything the super speed.

Huh?

這是什麼意思啊？

And one of my favorites came from a cake box given to the teachers once at an end-of-year celebration at school. The box was beautiful, with attractive pictures of cakes and goodies, with this written in elegant script:

另一個我覺得很有趣的例子是，有次在學校年終同樂會上送蛋糕給老師，盒子非常漂亮，上面印有精美的蛋糕和糖果的圖片，還有精緻的字體寫著 "The smell you'll never forget"。中

"The smell you'll never forget." In Chinese, they probably wanted to say, 你永遠也忘不了的香味, which sounds *great* in Chinese, but not in English!

In the years since, I have often joked about that saying with my children, but usually not in the context of delicious desserts!

Here are some great examples of mangled English. Note the funny name for the handicapped rest room. The menu below wants to sell "crab," but look what a difference just one letter makes! More of these jewels are online at www.engrish.com.

文原來可能想表達的是：「你永遠也忘不了的香味。」這在中文裡聽起來是很棒，但翻成英文卻變了個樣。

從那時候開始，我就經常用這句話來跟我的小孩開玩笑，只是並非用來形容美味的點心。

以下還有一些用錯英文的有趣例子，例如身障人士廁所上的爆笑用字，還有菜單上要賣 crab（螃蟹），卻因一字之差而造成天壤之別的差異。更多這種可笑的例子還可在 www.engrish.com 網站上觀賞。

www.picasaweb.google.com

www.engrish.com

www.engrish.com

www.engrish.com

www.engrish.com

Photo taken by the author at a Taiwan Freeway rest area, Summer of 2007

3 Better Writing Has Good Grammar and Spelling
正確的文法和拼字

Point three includes using **good grammar and spelling**. Also, there is a common misconception today. With spell and grammar check programs, some believe the computer will do all the work for you. Not so. There is still no substitute for knowing how to write clearly and well. Maybe you have seen this gem floating around on the Internet: it shows how spell checkers have their own flaws.

第三點是使用正確的文法和拼字。現在有些普遍的錯誤觀念，以為電腦上的拼字及文法檢查可以幫助你寫作，其實不然。沒有任何東西可以取代寫好作文的知識。也許你看過以下這首在網路上流傳已久的小詩，它證明了拼字檢查的功能仍有其限制。

A Little Poem Regarding Computer Spell Checkers...

Eye halve a spelling chequer
It came with my pea sea
It plainly marques four my revue
Miss steaks eye kin knot sea.

Eye strike a key and type a word
And weight four it two say
Weather eye am wrong oar write
It shows me strait a weigh.

As soon as a mist ache is maid
It nose bee fore two long
And eye can put the error rite
Its rare lea ever wrong.

Eye have run this poem threw it
I am shore your pleased two no
Its letter perfect awl the weigh
My chequer tolled me sew.

http://www.latech.edu/tech/liberal-arts/geography/courses/spellchecker.htm

This poem has <u>homophones</u>: words that sound the same but are spelled differently. So, even though each word above is spelled correctly, it is NOT the correct word for the meaning! This is how the poem *should* be spelled:

這首詩中有許多 homophones：也就是發音相同但拼法不同的字，因此就算每個字的拼法都正確，可是意義卻完全不對。這首詩的正確拼字如下：

> I have a spelling checker
> It came with my PC
> It plainly marks for my review
> Mistakes I cannot see.
>
> I strike a key and type a word
> And wait for it to say
> Whether I am wrong or right
> It shows me straight away.
>
> As soon as a mistake is made
> It knows before too long
> And I can put the error right
> It's rarely ever wrong.
>
> I have run this poem through it
> I am sure you're pleased to know
> It's letter perfect all the way
> My checker told me so.

4 Better Writing Considers Your Audience
考慮到讀者

A fourth part of better writing is considering **your audience**. What is the age of your audience? Their education? How much do they know about the topic? For example, knowing your audience helps you make decisions about word choice and sentence length. Are you writing a letter to the newspaper about the need for more parks in your town, or are you writing to a Ph.D. about nuclear power plants? Answer all these in your mind before writing, and keep reminding yourself that you are writing for *real people*. Try to make your writing clear and understandable for them. Some writers even try to envision the face of the reader, someone he or she knows, and *imagine writing—or even speaking—to that specific person*. You can try it; it may inspire you and help you personalize your writing.

精進寫作的第四點是考慮到讀者。讀者的年齡？教育程度？對主題的了解有多少？舉例來說，認識你的讀者可幫助你決定選用的字彙和句子長度。你是想寫信給報社建議在你住的城鎮興建更多公園？還是撰寫一封有關核能電廠的信給一名博士？在寫作前都要先在心裡思考這些問題，並且提醒自己，寫作的對象是活生生的人。努力讓你的文字清楚易懂，有些作者甚至會想像讀者的面貌，把讀者想成某個認識的人，然後想像是寫給那個人看，或說給那個人聽。你也可以試試看，這個技巧或許可以啟發你，讓你的寫作更具個人風格。

5 Better Writing is Patient
要有耐心

Point five is **patience**. We live in an impatient world. We have fast food and fast Internet. But writing is different. It takes time. Writing is also a process. Do not expect to sit down and create your masterpiece overnight. To get a good product, you must normally revise and revise. For instance, this book in July 2007 had 29 pages; by Christmas, it was up to 55; by January 1, 117; by Chinese New Year, 142. So when your teacher corrects your paper or suggests things to add or cut, please do not get upset. Your teacher just has some ideas to make your paper better. This reminds me of counsel from King Solomon: "Get all the advice you can and be wise the rest of your life." (Proverbs 19:20, *The Living Bible*)

And since we are on the topic of patience, here are the main steps in the Writing Process. (Note that the word *process* implies *many steps*!)

1. Prewriting 寫作前
Brainstorm about a topic; research; read widely; plan your writing. For more about this, see Step 1, "Start Strong," beginning on page 112.

2. Drafting 寫草稿
Create your outline; organize your thoughts; think of a good hook, conclusion, and what goes in the body of your paper. Just start writing, even if it seems sloppy. Writing with a computer lets you back up your

第五點是要有耐心。我們處在一個缺乏耐心的世界，從我們擁有的速食和快速網路就可以得知。然而寫作是不同的，它需要時間，它也是個過程。別奢望一坐下來就能信手寫出一篇大作。要寫出好的作品必須不斷修訂。例如你手上這本書在 2007 年 7 月時只有 29 頁，到了聖誕節時增加到 55 頁，在 1 月 1 日時是 117 頁，等到了中國農曆年就增加到 142 頁。所以當老師改正你的作文並建議增刪一些內容時，千萬不要不高興。你的老師只是提供意見來提升你的寫作品質。這讓我想到所羅門王的忠告：「你要聽勸教，受訓誨，使你終久有智慧。」（箴言第 19 章第 20 節，《當代聖經》）

既然我們談到耐心這個主題，以下是寫作過程的幾個主要步驟。（注意「過程」這個字就隱含需要眾多的步驟！）

針對一個題目腦力激盪、作些研究、廣泛閱讀、計畫如何寫作。更多資訊請看步驟一「有力的開始」(p. 112)。

擬出大綱、組織想法、想出一個吸引人的切入點、結論和文章的本體。只要放手去寫，有些凌亂也無妨。用電腦寫作可以讓你將文章儲存起來，之後要修改都很方便。等你完成初

masterpiece and it makes later correcting easier too. Once you have completed your first draft, you can edit.

稿,就可以開始編輯。

3. Editing/Proofreading 編輯／校訂

Look carefully for ways to improve flow, introductions, transitions, examples, etc. Search also for spelling or grammar mistakes. If possible, ask a friend—or even hire someone—to look over your paper. Remember: your paper makes perfect sense to *you*, because *you wrote it*. Another set of eyes will *almost always* find mistakes you overlooked. (See Step 12 on page 191, Finish with Formatting, for some common proofreading marks.)

仔細思考要如何改善文章的流暢度、概論、轉折、舉例等,同時也要檢查拼字和文法的錯誤。如果可能的話,請朋友或雇用某人來檢閱你的文章。要記住:讀自己的文章當然都是清楚無礙,因為那是你自己寫的。但請別人來看的話,幾乎都會找到你自己忽略的錯誤(請見第 191 頁的步驟 12:完稿前檢查格式,在此有一些常用的校訂符號。)

4. Publishing/Presenting 出版／發表

Get ready to go public with your paper, whether it is for a teacher, newspaper, or local garden club newsletter. And remember, with today's technology—websites, blogs, email—you can get your written message to a *global* audience in ways that people in the past could not even *dream* of...for free! But as the Bible teaches, with greater opportunity comes greater responsibility. If you are going to publish your work so that anyone in the world can read it, then be *extra certain* you approve of the content before you send it out. Once you hit "Send" or "Publish," you cannot recall it. Just ask one of the many people who has been fired because he wrote or forwarded an inappropriate email. Writing is far more permanent than speaking, so be careful what you put in print. Also, consider your *mood* when writing. Your emotions, whether happy or angry, can

要為公開自己的作品作準備,不論你是寫給老師、報社或當地園藝社的通訊。要記得:以現代的科技,不論是透過網站、部落格或電子郵件,你都能免費將訊息傳送給全世界的讀者,這是在過去所辦不到的。但就像聖經裡的教誨所說,機會愈多,責任就愈大。若是你想發表給全世界的人看,你就必須更加確信你傳送的內容是恰當的。一旦你按下「傳送」或「發表」,你就不能再召回這些文字。問問那些因為寫下或轉寄不恰當電子郵件而被解雇的人,你就知道其嚴重後果。白紙黑字比空口白話更能保存久遠,所以下筆為文要謹慎。另外,要注意寫作時的情緒,你的情緒不管是愉悅或氣憤,都很容易滲透到文字中,所以情緒波動時要慎於發表文章。當有疑慮時,先把作品放在一旁,等睡一覺,隔天早上再重讀,以確認這些文字

easily seep into your writing, so be careful of publishing when emotional. When in doubt, put your work aside, sleep on it one night, and reread it in the morning, to make certain that is what you truly want to say. King Solomon put it this way some 3,000 years ago: "A man of knowledge uses words with restraint." (Proverbs 17:27)

真的是你所想說的話。所羅門王在三千年前就說過：「寡少言語的，有知識。」（箴言第 17 章第 27 節）

One of the most famous documents in the Western world is the U.S. Declaration of Independence, written in 1776 by Virginian Thomas Jefferson, at the ripe age of 33. He was chosen as the main author because his peers knew he had a great way with words. Even so, his colleagues spent *three days* going through his product, adding this and cutting that. Jefferson endured the criticism, and we now know the final result: the U.S. declared its freedom from Britain. But look at the heavy editing!

西方世界最有名的文獻之一就是美國的〈獨立宣言〉，它是於 1776 年由來自維吉尼亞州的湯瑪斯‧傑佛遜在 33 歲的而立之年所撰寫。傑佛遜被挑選出來作為宣言的主要執筆者，因為他的同儕都知道他的文筆出色。即使如此，傑佛遜的同儕還是花了三天的時間來校閱他的作品，到處增修刪減。傑佛遜接受了這些批評，而我們現在都知道最終的成果：美國宣布脫離英國而獨立。但是你看看當時文件上大幅修訂的情況！

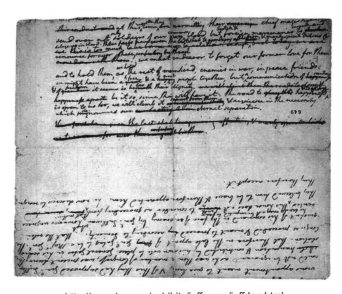

http://www.loc.gov/exhibits/jefferson/jeffdec.html

6 Better Writing Involves Reading Widely
廣泛閱讀

Point six is **read widely**: the more you read, the better you will write. One of the good things about being a parent is that you can learn some things you did *not* learn as a child. For instance, one night I was reading a book to my children about Benjamin Franklin (the man who graces the U.S. $100 bill), and learned that when Franklin was about twelve, he bought a subscription to the *Spectator*, the most famous British newspaper of his day. But he did not only read to learn the content, *he also actively read to understand how the authors crafted their articles.* Young Franklin would sometimes pick a favorite article, jot down some key points, wait a few days, and later try to rewrite the article in his own words. Then, he would reread the article and correct any mistakes he had made in his own version. Also as a lad, he would keep a daily journal; sometimes he would force himself to write his entries in rhyme, to make him improve his vocabulary. And all this at the age of twelve![1] Is it any wonder this fellow grew up to be one of the most famous authors in early America, and that his friends picked him to help Jefferson write the Declaration of Independence?

Young Franklin knew a secret. By reading, you can mimic and learn from your favorite authors. This does *not* mean you try to become a Xerox® copy of someone else. As I said above, your writing is an extension of *you*. Still, we *can* all learn from authors we greatly

第六點是廣泛閱讀：你閱讀的書愈多，寫作能力就愈佳。身為父母的好處之一就是可以重新學習你在童年時未曾學過的東西。舉例來說，有天晚上我讀一本有關班哲明·富蘭克林（也就是使一百元美鈔更加美觀的肖像人物）的書給我的小孩聽，我才知道當富蘭克林 12 歲時，他就已經訂閱當時最有名的英國報紙《觀察者》。而且他不只是閱讀內容而已，他還主動去了解那些作者如何寫作。年輕的富蘭克林有時會挑一篇他喜歡的文章，記下一些重點，過幾天後再用自己的文字重寫。接著他再重讀原先那篇文章並訂正自己寫作上的錯誤。同時他也會寫日記，有時會強迫自己在寫作時要押韻，以增進自己用字的能力。這一切都是在他 12 歲時做的事。也難怪這小傢伙長大後會成為美國早期最有名的作家之一，而他的朋友更推舉他協助傑佛遜撰寫〈獨立宣言〉。

年輕的富蘭克林知道一個祕訣，透過閱讀你可以模仿學習你最喜歡的作家。這並不是叫你成為影印機去拷貝別人，而是如我之前所說的，你的寫作應該是你的延伸。然而，我們仍可學習我們所崇敬的作家，注意他

---

1 Fleming, Candace. *Ben Franklin's Almanac: Being a True Account of the Good Gentleman's Life.* Simon & Schuster, New York: 2003.

enjoy. Note how they craft their arguments, arrange their sentences, and choose their words. Save favorite articles. Look for "writing heroes" and find ways to learn from them, yet keep your own individuality.

Please allow me a final word about reading widely. I have taught thousands of students in both the U.S. and Taiwan, and it becomes quite clear which students read often and which do not. Those who read widely have better word choice, more fluency, and more in-depth knowledge of subjects. In contrast, those students who seldom read have shallower understanding of the material and poorer writing and speaking skills. Those who love to read always have the competitive edge. A good friend and Chinese teacher of mine, Richard, was a fine example of this. When I met Richard, I thought that he had lived in the U.S. for years; not only did he speak with an American accent, but he also had excellent word choice and even knew English idioms and when to use them. You can imagine my shock when I learned *he had never left Taiwan*! He was truly gifted with languages, but he also had a secret: he read English each night before bed. And he did not read English textbooks; he read native-speaker materials. One of his favorites was *Reader's Digest* (a great resource for learning English). Of course all this reading took time, but Richard knew that there is no shortcut to success.

們是如何論證、鋪陳句子和選擇字彙。你可以保存喜愛的文章，尋找你的「寫作英雄」，思考如何從他們身上學習，但是仍保有你的主體性。

我再說一些有關廣泛閱讀的事，我在美國和台灣教過無數的學生，我很容易看出哪些學生經常閱讀，哪些不常閱讀。廣泛閱讀的學生用字較精確、寫作較流暢、對主題具備較深入的知識。相對地，不常閱讀的學生對教材的理解較淺薄、寫作和口語的技巧也較差。喜愛閱讀的學生總是具有競爭優勢。舉例來說，我有一名教我中文的台灣好朋友，名叫 Richard。我第一次和他見面時，還以為他在美國居住過很多年。他不僅有美國口音，而且精通英文用字和成語。當我知道他從未離開過台灣時，你可以想像我有多訝異！他的確有語言天份，但他更有個祕訣：他每晚睡前都會讀英文。他不是讀英文課本，而是讀英語母語人士讀的書，包括他最喜歡的《讀者文摘》（是學習英文的絕佳資源）。當然讀這些書是很花時間，但 Richard 知道成功是沒有捷徑的。

7 Better Writing Chooses a Good Place and Time to Write
適當的時間和地點

Here is a brief suggestion about <u>Point Seven</u>, ***where you should write***. First, have a dictionary and thesaurus available to help you with word choice. To get off to a strong start, pick a good spot to concentrate, preferably one that is well-lit, comfortable, and quiet, with few distractions or interruptions. In our digital age, this is getting harder to do, so I suggest you turn off the TV, radio, and cell phone. As a father of four children, ages ten to thirteen, I struggle to find quiet. So, when my parents said they were going out of town after Christmas and that I could stay at their place for a few days to write this book, I jumped at the chance. The extended blocks of quiet, uninterrupted time are great for writing. And if you *cannot* find those big blocks of quiet time? Just grab what time you can, 20 minutes here, an hour there. Some find early morning the best time to write; others, late at night.

再來是有關第七點的建議：你應該在何處寫作。首先要準備好字典和辭典來幫你選擇字彙。為了要有個好的開始，先挑個可以集中精神、最好是光線充足、舒適安靜的地方，才不會有太多的干擾。在數位時代裡，這種地方愈來愈難找，所以我建議你關掉電視、收音機和手機。身為一名有四個年紀從 10 歲至 13 歲的小孩的父親，就很難找到清靜之處。所以當我的父母表示他們在聖誕節後要出城一陣子，而我可以待在他們家幾天來寫這本書時，我忙不迭的就答應了。能有長期不受打擾的安靜時光對寫作而言真是太棒了。但如果你無法空出一大段安靜的時刻，那就把握你擁有的任何片刻時間，也許這兒 20 分鐘，那邊一小時。有人覺得清晨是寫作的最佳時機，有人則偏愛在半夜筆耕。

The "Magical Seven" Structures of Classroom Writing

課堂寫作的魔法七結構

We now shift our focus from some traits of better writing to some of the different *kinds* of writing. Please understand there are <u>many different kinds of writing styles and purposes</u>. Here we will look at a few of the more common types, the kinds your teacher will likely assign you. This section has brief descriptions and explanations, plus real examples from Taiwan undergraduate university students' essays, with some comments and suggestions.

現在我們把焦點從精進寫作的特點轉移到不同形式的寫作。其實寫作有各種風格和目的，以下我們會探討幾種常見的寫作形式，也就是你的老師常出的作文題目。以下這章包括簡短的描述和解釋，並以台灣的大學生所寫的作文爲例，再加上一些評論和建議。

1 Description
描述文

In this style, you are describing someone or something. One trick here is to try to <u>involve the five senses</u> when you write. For instance, let's say you wanted to write about a summer day. This is dull: "It was a very hot day so I sat outside and had a drink."

這種風格是要求你描述某人或某物。其中一個技巧就是讓五種感官的感受融入文字裡。例如你要描寫夏天，只寫「這是個大熱天，所以我坐在屋外喝飲料。」就顯得很呆板。

Instead, try this: "It was a hot day—about 35°C, and my T-shirt was damp with sweat—so I found a shady spot under a banyan tree. It was like sitting under a gigantic green umbrella. I had just bought a milk tea, and the cup felt cool to my fingers. A slight breeze of fresh, country air stirred across my face. In the branches

你可以試著這樣寫：「這是個大熱天，約有攝氏 35 度，汗水浸濕了我的 T 恤，所以我在榕樹下找了一個遮蔭處，就好像坐在一把巨大的綠傘下。我剛買了杯奶茶，杯子的冰涼直透指尖。鄉間清新的微風吹拂過臉龐，頭上樹枝間傳來陣陣的鳥鳴聲。啊～生命眞是美好！」

above, I heard a few birds chirping. Ah...life is good!"

Look at the senses you invoked:

細數一下你所喚起的感受：

Touch: damp T-shirt, cool cup, slight breeze across your face	觸覺：濕透的T恤、冰涼的杯子、吹拂過臉龐的微風
Taste: delicious milk tea	味覺：美味的奶茶
Sound: birds chirping	聽覺：鳥鳴聲
Smell: fresh, country air	嗅覺：清新的鄉間空氣
Sight: tree, like a green umbrella	視覺：像把綠傘的大樹

See, this short passage touches on <u>all five senses</u>!

看到了嗎？這短短的幾行字就觸發了所有的五種感官！

The next is a collection of real, Taiwan university student work. You will find three copies of each essay. Draft 1 is what the students gave their professor. Draft 2 has my editing and comments. Draft 3 is the revised essay, with my editing built in. This valuable section is here to let you see actual student work and some specific editing to make it clearer and smoother.

接下來是台灣的大學生所撰寫的作文，每篇作文有三個版本。第一個版本是學生交給教授的作業，第二個版本加上了我的修訂和評語，第三個是修訂後的版本。本章非常重要，你可以看到學生的實際作品，以及如何使這些作品更加清晰流暢的修訂方式。

Below is our first article, originally entitled "Hot Weather."

以下是第一篇作文，原本的題目是「炎熱的天氣」。

Draft 1

Hot Weather

In recent years, the problem about climate warms up becomes more and more serious. Hot weather has many bad influences on the environment and human body. There are three effects as follows: the disappearance of iceberg, an unusual change in global climate, a decrease in people's powers of concentration.

To begin with, due to temperature increase, the iceberg will melt. As all of us know, the polar bear's natural habitat is Arctic iceberg. Because the iceberg melts, their habitat will be deprived of. If polar bears lose their habitat, they will face to the endangered plight. Next, the global climate will become unusual as a result of the increased heat. Since the weather is getting hotter and hotter, living creatures on the earth will be unbearable to the heat. For instance, poikilothermal animals like crocodiles don't have the function to regulate the body temperature; therefore, they will probably die out because they can't endure the external temperature. Moreover, it's hard for common people to apt to such heat; to say nothing of people who live in tropic or desert—maybe they will be hot to death. Last, owing to the hot weather, it becomes more difficult for people to pay attention to things. Heat will make people absent-minded as well as drowsy. Consequently, people will be slow in reaction and the working efficiency will lower.

Now, here is the same passage, with my editing comments. Items I cut are marked through; items added are in blue. Explanatory comments are in the margin.

接下來，同樣的文章加上我的修訂和評語。刪除的部分畫刪除線，增添的部分以藍色字表示，解釋性的評語則置於旁邊空白處。

Draft 2

~~Hot Weather~~ Burning Up

▸ The title "Hot Weather" is rather boring.

In recent years, the problem ~~about~~ of climate ~~warms up~~ change has ~~becomes~~ more and more serious. Specifically, many areas show increases in temperature. ~~Hot~~ Extreme hot weather has many bad influences on the environment and human body. ~~There are three effects as follows:~~ This paper will consider three specific aspects: the disappearance of many icebergs, an unusual change in global climate, and a decrease in people's powers of concentration.

▸ I added this sentence to show that the kind of climate change we are dealing with is heat.

▸ "Icebergs" must be plural, because we are not talking about just one iceberg.

▸ Use "and" when you get to the last item in a series.

To begin with, due to temperature increases, ~~the~~ many icebergs will melt. As all of us know, the polar bear's natural habitat is the tundra and Arctic icebergs. ~~Because the~~ When icebergs melts, however, polar bears lose a crucial part of their habitat ~~will be deprived of.~~ If polar bears lose their habitat, they ~~will face to the~~ may become endangered plight or even extinct. Next

▸ Do not use passive voice.

~~Second~~, *Second,* the global climate will become ~~unusual~~ *change* as a result of the increased heat. Since the weather *in many areas* is getting hotter and hotter, living *some* creatures on the earth ~~will be unbearable to the heat~~ *may not be able to adjust and survive.* For instance, ~~poikilothermal animals~~ *cold-blooded reptiles* like crocodiles don't have the function to ~~do not~~ regulate their body temperature; therefore, they ~~will probably~~ *may* die out because they ~~can't~~ *cannot* endure the external temperature. Moreover, ~~it's~~ *it is* hard for common people to ~~apt to~~ *handle* such *extreme* heat~~;~~*,* to say nothing of people who live in *the* tropics or desert—~~maybe they will be hot to death~~ *the heat there may prove fatal.* ~~Last~~ *Finally,* ~~owing to~~ *because of* the hot weather, it becomes more difficult for people to pay attention to things. Heat will make people absent-minded as well as drowsy. Consequently, people will be *have* slower in reaction *times* and their working efficiency will be lower. *Clearly, climate change is an issue that deserves our study and attention; we should all do what we can to help protect the environment.*

> To make your writing clearer, use "first," "second," etc., not just "next."

> Avoid obscure words—just call them "cold-blooded."

> Avoid contractions.

> "Hot to death" is Chinglish.

> Avoid "owing to." Although many people write it, it sounds awkward.

> Note how the first essay ended with "efficiency will be lower." That is too sudden. The paper needs some conclusion, even if just one sentence.

Below is Draft 3, with the corrections built in.　　最後這一篇是修訂後的完整版本。

Draft 3

Burning Up

In recent years, the problem of climate change has become more and more serious. Specifically, many areas show increases in temperature. Extreme hot weather has many bad influences on the environment and human body. This paper will consider three specific aspects: the disappearance of many icebergs, an unusual change in global climate, and a decrease in people's powers of concentration.

To begin with, due to temperature increases, many icebergs will melt. As all of us know, the polar bear's natural habitat is the tundra and Arctic icebergs. When icebergs melt, however, polar bears lose a crucial part of their habitat. If polar bears lose their habitat, they may become endangered or even extinct. Second, the global climate will change as a result of the increased heat. Since the weather in many areas is getting hotter, some creatures may not be able to adjust and survive. For instance, cold-blooded reptiles like crocodiles do not regulate their body temperature; therefore, they may die out because they cannot endure the external temperature. Moreover, it is hard for common people to handle extreme heat, to say nothing of people who live in the tropics or desert—the heat there may prove fatal. Finally, because of the hot weather, it becomes more difficult for people to pay attention to things. Heat will make people absent-minded as well as drowsy. Consequently, people will have slower reaction times and their working efficiency will be lower. Clearly, climate change is an issue that deserves our study and attention; we should all do what we can to help protect the environment.

Description can cover things (like climate change), or places, or people. Below is another description essay; it reports on an interview with Cathy², a student at National Taipei University (NTPU). Here is the original paper.

描述文可以描述事物（如天氣變化）、地方或人物。以下是另一篇描述文，記述與一名台北大學的學生 Cathy 的訪談內容。第一篇是學生原本的作文。

Draft 1

Cathy

The person I interviewed today is Cathy. She studies in the English department of NTPU, and her other major is law.

English is very important to her. In high school, she always got good grades on that subject. Therefore, she picked English as her major, and entered NTPU. She thinks the advantage of studying at NTPU is that there are all sorts of new equipment on campus. However, one of the downsides is that this college is located in the southern part of Taipei; it is too far away from her home. She has to spend a lot of time on transportation everyday. What is more, this university is still under construction, several departments must be built in order for it to be completed. She can not bear the fact that a college has no library or gym. These two defects make her feel disappointed in NTPU.

The reason she chose English composition is because she wants to improve her English writing skills. She hopes to write as well as English native speakers do.

Finally, at the end of the conversation, I asked her about her future plans. She said that because she is taking law courses, she hopes she can study law abroad. She laughed and said, "In order to fulfill my dream, I

---

2 Not her real name.

have to study harder in the law department from now on!" She is such a diligent girl. I hope one day I can see her dream comes true.

Here is the revised essay, with editing.　　　　　以下是修訂過的文章。

Draft 2

Cathy The Law Student Who Loves English

The person I interviewed today is Cathy. She studies in the English department of NTPU, and her other major is law.

English is very important to her. In high school, she always got *earned* good grades on *in* that subject., Therefore, *so* she picked English as her major, and entered NTPU. She thinks the *biggest* advantage of studying at NTPU is that there are all sorts *the wide array* of new equipment on campus. However, one of the downsides is that this college is located in the southern part of Taipei;, it is too far away from her home. She has to spend a lot of time *many hours* on transportation *the road* everyday *every day*. What is more, this university is still under construction,; several

> ▶ The second title is a little long but I think it is better. If your name is Cathy please don't take this the wrong way, but I think the original title is a little dull.

> ▶ This is vague: the author should give us a few examples of new equipment that students like.

> ▶ Vague: tell us how much time.

> ▶ This is a common error: "every day" means "each day," while "everyday" is an adjective, meaning normal or common, like "everyday problems."

> ▶ You need a semi-colon here because you are joining two independent clauses.

departments must be built in order for it to be completed. She ~~can not~~ *cannot* bear the fact that a college has no library or gym. These two defects make her feel disappointed in NTPU.

The reason she chose English composition *class* is because ~~that~~ she wants to improve her English writing skills. She hopes to *someday* write as well as English native speakers *of English* do.

Finally, at the end of the conversation, I asked her about her future plans. She said ~~that because she is taking law courses,~~ she hopes ~~she can~~ *to* study law abroad. She laughed and said, "In order to fulfill my dream, I have to study harder in the law department from now on!" She is such a diligent ~~girl~~ *young lady*. I hope one day I can see her ~~dreams~~ comes true.

To English speakers, "girl" usually brings images of someone under, say, 13 or 14.

And finally, here is the essay with the corrections embedded.   最後是修訂完成的版本。

Draft 3

The Law Student Who Loves English

The person I interviewed today is Cathy. She studies in the English department of NTPU and her other major is law.

English is very important to her. In high school she always earned good grades in that subject, so she picked English as her major and entered NTPU. She thinks the biggest advantage of studying at NTPU is the wide array of new equipment on campus. However, one of the downsides is that this college is located in the southern part of Taipei, far away from her home. She has to spend many hours on the road every day. What is more, this university is still under construction; several departments must be built in order for it to be completed. She cannot bear the fact that a college has no library or gym. These two defects make her feel disappointed in NTPU.

The reason she chose English composition class is that she wants to improve her English writing skills. She hopes to someday write as well as native speakers of English do.

Finally, at the end of the conversation, I asked about her future plans. She said she hopes to study law abroad. She laughed and said, "In order to fulfill my dream, I have to study harder in the law department from now on!" She is such a diligent young lady. I hope one day I can see her dreams come true.

2 Narration
敘述文

Narration is just telling a story, real or imagined. To be clear, organize your paper, usually in chronological order.

敘述文是訴說一個真實或想像的故事。為了要表達清楚，通常是以時間的先後次序來組織文章。

Here is an example in its original form of a narration from a Taiwan university student. I like how this story has a strong chronological order, a clear list of factors that led to the crash, and helpful lessons to draw from the experience. (This story also has elements of Cause and Effect, which we will look at later.)

以下是一名台灣的大學生所寫的一篇敘述文，我喜歡這個故事有很清楚的時間順序，很清楚地呈現導致意外的一連串的因素，並從此經驗中獲得有益的教訓。（這個故事具有因果關係的要素，這在後面的章節會談到。）

Draft 1

The Bicycle and the Accident

I remember that it was a rainy day and the accident occurred in the afternoon. After school, I gave Cynthia a ride back to the dormitory. She sat behind me and held an umbrella for us. On the way to the dormitory, we chatted and had some snacks. When we rode near the dormitory, I made a turn on an iron board. All of a sudden, we tumbled off the bicycle and directly hit the ground.

While we went into our dormitory, we were in a bad mood. On thinking of the looks we got from others, we felt embarrassed and decided to examine the causes.

The direct cause is absolutely the iron board because the rain made it slippery. Moreover, Cynthia had a heavy backpack. Thus, the back part of the bike was heavier than the front. That means, when I turned the bicycle, the back weight seemed to drag me and made me lose control of the bicycle. Besides, the umbrella and snacks may be another reason. As I rode the bicycle, Cynthia had to hold the umbrella in one hand and snacks in the other hand. As a result, she couldn't keep balance well behind me; when I made a turn, our weight caused us to lean to one side and made the bicycle turned over. In addition, the narrow tires of the bicycle contributed to the accident as well. They were too narrow to support our weight when confronted with the sudden momentum. Therefore, when we stood up from the ground, we found that one tire became deformed. If the tires were broader, we could have passed the iron board without falling down because they could be strong and stable and would support us.

What's more, our weight could also give rise to the accident. Our total weight was near one hundred kilograms, so the light bike couldn't bear our heavy weight, which becomes a dangerous factor. Furthermore, my riding skill is not good and mature enough. While I was riding, I couldn't pay attention to the environment because I was looking around to see more sights on the way. Consequently, the accident took place.

By this accident, we learned a lesson that when we are riding bikes, we should pay more attention to the environment especially in bad weather and notice whether the bike could bear the total weight on it. The more circumspect we are under all kinds of considered conditions, the safer we will be when really confronted with hazards.

Now here is the article, with corrections. Again, some items are cut; added items are in blue; explanatory comments are in the margin.

以下的文章有加上修正部分。有些字被刪除了，新增的字以藍色表示，解釋性評語置於旁邊空白處。

Draft 2

The Bicycle and the Accident The Bike Accident

→ shorter, stronger title

I remember that it It was a rainy day and the accident occurred in the afternoon when we had the bike accident. After school class, I gave Cynthia a ride back to the dormitory. She sat behind me and held an umbrella for us. On the way to the dormitory, we chatted and had some snacks. When we rode near But as we neared the dormitory, I made a turned on an iron board a steel plate that was in the road surface. All of a sudden Suddenly, we tumbled off the bicycle and directly hit the ground.

→ Look for ways to make verbs out of nouns.

→ By using "Suddenly," you can cut three words.

While When we went into our dormitory, we were both in a bad mood. On thinking of the looks we got from others, we We felt embarrassed and decided to examine the causes of our misfortune.

The direct cause of our crash is was absolutely the

~~iron board~~ steel plate because the rain made it slippery. Moreover, Cynthia had a heavy backpack. ~~Thus~~ So, the back part of the bike was heavier than the front. That means, when I turned the bicycle, the back weight seemed to drag me and made me lose control of the bicycle. Besides, ~~the~~ holding the umbrella and snacks ~~may be another reason~~ did not make controlling the bike any easier. As I rode the bicycle, Cynthia had to hold the umbrella in one hand and snacks in the other hand. As a result, she ~~couldn't~~ could not keep her balance well ~~behind me~~; when I made a the turn, our weight caused us to lean to one side and made the bicycle turned over. ~~In addition, the~~ The bike's narrow tires ~~of the bicycle~~ contributed to the accident as well. They were too narrow to support our weight when confronted with the sudden momentum. ~~Therefore, when~~ When we stood up ~~from the ground~~ after the crash, we found that one tire ~~became~~ had become ~~deformed~~ warped. If the tires ~~were~~ had been broader, maybe we could have ~~passed~~ ridden over the ~~iron board~~ steel plate without falling down because they could be strong and stable ~~and would~~ enough to support us.

→ Saying "In addition" and "as well" is redundant.

→ Use active voice.

What's more Furthermore, our combined weight could also give have given rise to the accident. Our total weight was nearly one hundred kilograms, so the light bike couldn't could not bear our heavy weight, which becomes a dangerous factor load. Besides, my riding skill is not good and mature enough I am not a really good biker. While I was riding, I couldn't did not pay close attention to the environment my surroundings because I was too busy looking around to see more sights on the way at all the sights. Consequently, the accident took place. For all these reasons, we crashed.

By From this accident, we learned a valuable lesson: that when we are riding bikes, we should pay more close attention to the environment our surroundings, especially in bad weather and notice whether the bike could can bear the total weight on it. The more circumspect careful we are under all kinds of considered conditions, the safer we will be when really confronted with hazards.

> Note how you can usually say more with fewer words. The last sentence originally had 21 words; it now has just 14.

Finally, here is the narration, with corrections built in.   最後，修正完成的敘述文如下：

Draft 3

The Bike Accident

It was a rainy afternoon when we had the bike accident. After class, I gave Cynthia a ride back to the dormitory. She sat behind me and held an umbrella for us. On the way to the dorm, we chatted and had some snacks. But as we neared the dorm, I turned on a steel plate that was in the road surface. Suddenly, we tumbled off the bicycle and hit the ground.

When we went into our dormitory, we were both in a bad mood. We felt embarrassed and decided to examine the causes of our misfortune.

The direct cause of our crash was the steel plate because the rain made it slippery. Moreover, Cynthia had a heavy backpack. So, the back part of the bike was heavier than the front. That means, when I turned the bicycle, the back weight seemed to drag me and made me lose control of the bicycle. Besides, holding the umbrella and snacks did not make controlling the bike any easier. As I rode the bicycle, Cynthia had to hold the umbrella in one hand and snacks in the other. As a result, she could not keep her balance well; when I made the turn, our weight caused us to lean to one side and made the bicycle turn over. The bike's narrow tires contributed to the accident as well. They were too narrow to support our weight when confronted with the sudden momentum. When we stood up after the crash, we found that one tire had become warped. If the tires had been broader, maybe we could have ridden over the steel plate without falling down because they could be strong and stable enough to support us.

Furthermore, our combined weight could also have given rise to the accident. Our total weight was nearly one hundred kilograms, so the light bike could not bear our heavy load. Furthermore, I am not a really good biker. While I was riding, I did not pay close attention to my surroundings because I was too busy looking around at all the sights. For all these reasons, we crashed.

From this accident we learned a valuable lesson: when we are riding bikes, we should pay close attention to our surroundings, especially in bad weather and notice whether the bike can bear the total weight. The more careful we are, the safer we will be when confronted with hazards.

3 How-to Papers
「如何」類文章

This common paper involves a simple step-by-step process about how to do or make something. The humble cookbook is nothing more than a collection of how-to papers. Here too, organization is everything. Find some way to make your steps crystal clear for your reader. A common format goes something like this:

1. Introduce your topic and why it is important.
2. Explain what materials or preparation you need beforehand.
3. Explain the process step-by-step. Use numbers or letters to make the steps clear.
4. Conclude your paper.

For example, here is a recipe I found in my Mom's kitchen. It is crystal clear.

這類常見的文體是有關如何從事或製作某種事物的簡易步驟。例如簡單的食譜書就只不過是一些如何動手做的文章集合。同樣地，組織性是最重要的。力求讓每個步驟清晰，讀者才可輕鬆理解。一個常用的模式如下：

1. 介紹題目和它的重要性。

2. 解釋事先需要何種材料和準備事項。

3. 解釋過程的每個步驟，使用數字或字母清楚標示這些步驟。

4. 為全文作結語。

例如以下這份食譜是我在母親的廚房找到的，非常清楚易懂。

Fresh Snow Peas with Pork

Try it tonight! This savory classic helps your body maintain normal blood pressure *and* fends off any tendency to diabetes. It is also an excellent pick-me-up whenever you need extra energy.

Ingredients:

⅓ pound (150 g) fresh snow peas

⅓ pound (150 g) lean pork

2 tablespoons (30 ml) of cooking wine

1 teaspoon (10 cc) of salt

2 tablespoons (30 ml) of cornstarch

2 tablespoons (30 ml) of vegetable oil

1 ½ cups (355 ml) of water

Directions:

1. Cut lean pork into short, thin slices.
2. Combine ½ teaspoon salt with the cornstarch, cooking wine, and ½ cup (118 ml) water. Mix well and let stand.
3. Boil the snow peas in boiling water for 6 minutes. Drain and let stand.
4. Heat the vegetable oil in wok or sauté pan over high heat. Add the pork slices and stir continuously for 3 minutes.
5. Add 1 cup (237 ml) of water. Then add the snow peas, cornstarch mixture, the remaining ½ teaspoon of salt, and cook for another 5 minutes.
6. You are done! Remove from stove and serve.

Do you see how the clear introduction makes this recipe attractive? Also, the list of ingredients and numbered instructions make it easy to follow.

Now, just for fun, imagine this recipe written as a *paragraph, without* the numbers. It is a nightmare! <u>Never</u> write like this!

你有發現清楚的介紹可以讓這份食譜讀起來更吸引人嗎？而且將食材列表和烹調步驟條列可以讓人更容易了解。

以下純屬娛樂，想像一下把這份食譜寫成一個段落，不用條列分項，讀起來就很可怕吧！千萬不要寫成這樣。

Fresh Snow Peas with Pork

The first thing you need to do is cut lean pork into short, thin slices. (You will need about ⅓ pound (150 g) of lean pork.) Next, combine ½ teaspoon (5 cc) salt with 2 tablespoons (30 ml) of cornstarch, 2 tablespoons (30 ml) of cooking wine, and ½ cup (118 ml) of water. Mix these ingredients well and let stand. (You will call this the cornstarch mixture.) Next, boil ⅓ pound (150 g) of fresh snow peas in boiling water. Boil them for 6 minutes. Next, drain them and let them stand. Next, heat 2 tablespoons (30 ml) of vegetable oil in a wok or sauté pan over high heat. Next, add the pork slices and keep stirring for 3 minutes. Next, add 1 cup (237 ml) of water. Next, add ⅓ pound (150 g) of snow peas, cornstarch mixture, the remaining ½ teaspoon (5 cc) salt, and cook for another 5 minutes. Next, remove pan from heat to serve the dish. Finally, you can eat it!

Here is a student's how-to paper about a common yet crucial issue: How to make friends. We live in a world where email and cell phone technology make it easier than ever to communicate with people; sadly, however, it seems more and more people feel disconnected and friendless.

以下是一名同學的「如何」類文章，寫一個很平常但又很重要的題目：如何交朋友。生活中的電子郵件及手機等科技，使我們在與人溝通上能享受前所未有的便利。但很可惜，似乎也有愈來愈多的人覺得失聯和缺乏朋友。

This author does a fine job: the paper is short but rich in meaningful content. Also, even though this paper does not lend itself to the "1, 2, 3" format of a recipe, it still has clear organization based on "first," "second," and "finally." Here is the original paper.

這個作者寫得還不錯：文章雖然短，但內容豐富而有意義。儘管這篇文章並沒有像食譜一樣列出「1, 2, 3」等步驟，但它的組織仍是遵循「第一」、「第二」和「最後」的順序。以下是原本同學寫的文章：

Draft 1

Making Friends

Friend is a valuable treasure in life, therefore it is important to know how to "make friends." To build friendship is not an easy task; however, there are still some traces we can follow to make friends. First of all, you have to take the initiative in making acquaintances. Never bind yourself in your own little circle; it will only make yourself isolated form others. Second, you should remember always bring your smiling face with you when meeting people. It is obvious that no one wants to come near a person with a fearful face. One little smile will break the ice between people and make others think that you are an easygoing person. Finally, you should try to be considerate. Being considerate is not telling you to be too finicky about everything you do; just that you should think before you do some sensitive action. Since impulse action may easily hurt other's feelings, you should be careful with what you say or do. These three tips are only a rough guideline for everyone, but they are the basic rules. Remember these three points and try to do your best to develop your own friendship.

Here is the paper again, with a few editing points.

以下是同樣的文章，再加上一些修訂的重點。

Draft 2

Making Friends

Friends is are a valuable treasure in life, therefore so it is important to know how to "make friends." To build Building friendships is not an easy task; however,

→ *"Therefore" sounds too formal for this usage here.*

→ *Do not overuse quotation marks.*

there are still some traces *principles* we can follow to make friends. First of all, ~~you have to~~ take the initiative in making acquaintances. Never bind yourself in your own little circle; it will only make yourself isolated ~~form~~ *from* others. Second, ~~you should~~ remember *to* always bring your ~~smiling face~~ *smile* ~~with you~~ when meeting people. ~~It is obvious that~~ *Clearly,* no one wants to come near a person with a ~~fearful~~ *grim* face. One little smile will break the ice between people and make others think that you are an easygoing person. Finally, ~~you should try~~ to be considerate. Being considerate is *does* ~~not telling you to be too finicky~~ *mean being hyper-sensitive* about everything you do; ~~it~~ just *means* that you should think before you *say* or ~~do some sensitive action~~ *something*. Since ~~impulse~~ *impulsive* action*s* may easily hurt ~~other's~~ *others'* feelings, ~~you should be careful with what you say or do.~~ These three tips are only a rough guideline for everyone, but they are the basic rules. Remember these three points and try to do your best to develop your own friendship*s*.

▸ This is a good example of a spelling error that spell-check will not find. "Form" and "from" are both words.

▸ Cut the "you should" and "you have to" and go right to the verb.

▸ Just say "smile." "Smiling face" is Chinglish.

▸ Here we replaced 4 words with one.

And finally, here is the essay, with corrections built in.   以下是加入修訂後的版本。

Draft 3

Making Friends

Friends are a valuable treasure in life, so it is important to know how to make friends. Building friendships is not an easy task; however, there are still some principles we can follow to make friends. First of all, take the initiative in making acquaintances. Never bind yourself in your own little circle; it will only make you isolated from others. Second, remember to always bring your smile when meeting people. Clearly, no one wants to come near a person with a grim face. One little smile will break the ice between people and make others think that you are an easygoing person. Finally, be considerate. Being considerate does not mean being hyper-sensitive about everything you do; it just means that you should think before you say or do something. Since impulsive actions may easily hurt others' feelings, be careful with what you say or do. These three tips are only a rough guideline for everyone, but they are the basic rules. Remember these three points and do your best to develop your own friendships.

4 Definition
定義

This kind of paper lets you define a term or word. At first this may sound easy but it is not. In English as in any language, one word may often have several different definitions or connotations. For example, note how the word *conservative* is used below:

這類文章是請你定義一個詞或字，聽起來好像很簡單，但其實不然。在英文或其他語言中，一個字通常有幾種不同的定義或義涵。例如 conservative 就有以下幾種用法：

> A. My grandmother is so conservative; she seldom accepts any new ideas.
>
> B. Please be conservative with the paper cups; we only have a few and we do not want to run out at the picnic.
>
> C. It is wise to choose conservative dress for a job interview.

Do you see the difference? In A, conservative means traditional or the opposite of liberal; in B it means careful or the opposite of wasteful, while in C it means professional and not flashy. And not only are the definitions different, but the connotation, or the *flavor* of the word, is also different. Sentence A has a very negative tone, judging conservative as a vice, while B praises conservative as a virtue.

你看得出它們的差異嗎？A 句中 conservative 指傳統的或守舊的；B 句意謂小心的或節省的；C 句則是專業或保守的。不只是定義不同，連義涵或韻味也不一樣。A 句有強烈否定的語氣，認爲 conservative 是不好的；B 句中的 conservative 則被視爲是一種美德。

Now let us look at it from another angle. Suppose you are describing your friend, Barbara, who is very thin.

現在讓我們換個角度來看，假設你要描述你的朋友 Barbara 是個非常瘦的人。

> A. Barbara is thin.
>
> B. Barbara is skinny.
>
> C. Barbara is scrawny.
>
> D. Barbara is petite.
>
> E. Barbara is slender.

On the one hand, you are saying the same thing: Barbara is not large. However, look at the *tone* of each word. Sentence A is basically neutral, sentences B and especially C are negative, while D and especially E are positive.

You can see how defining carefully and choosing just the right word are so important for writers. Author Mark Twain once said, "The difference between the right word and the almost right word is the difference between lighting and a lighting bug." Know your words and use them well.

Here is a definition essay from a university student in Taipei.

在某方面而言，你都是在描述同樣的事情：Barbara 並不胖。但是每個字的語氣都有差別。A 句基本上是中性的寫法，B 句和 C 句是負面的，而 D 句和 E 句則是正面的。

你可以看出小心下定義和選擇正確用字對寫作者有多重要。作家馬克·吐溫曾說：「正確用字和幾乎正確用字的差別，就好像閃電和螢火蟲的差別。」所以要認清字義並謹慎使用。

以下是台北的一名同學所寫的定義類文章。

Draft 1

My Definition of a Successful College Student

What quality does a successful college student have to possess? When one is admitted to enter a college, what should he have if he wants to play a role of a successful college student? A college student has more chances to get along with different people than before. Due to the fact that college time is a period that connects the school life and social life, what lie in front of them is that they need to prepared themselves for stepping into the adult society; as a result, I think it is necessary for a successful college student to have two vital ability: the ability to solve problems he meets and the ability to learn new knowledge.

Solving problems sounds simple, but actually it is not a easy task. When we meet a problem, what should we do? Some people will flee from it while a successful college student should not do that. Indeed, he should face it and deal with it because he is no longer a neophyte who first experiences problems. He should know how to handle and make decisions while facing a problem since a college student is old enough to be his own master.

Secondly, being a future member of varied career fields, a successful college student must possess the ability to learn new knowledge. This ability would assist you to keep in touch with the easy-to-change world. In this world, the information is flashing and knowledge is often updating; hence, to survive and succeed in this world, a college student must become familiar with new knowledge.

In conclusion, in my opinion, a successful college student should possess the ability to solve problems and the ability to learn new knowledge both. That would distinguish you from a group of ordinary college students.

Here is the same essay, with editing.   以下是附上修訂的文章。

Draft 2

My Definition of a Successful College Student

What quality *qualities* does a successful college student have *need* to possess? When one is admitted to enter a college, what should he have if he wants

▸ Or, you can simply entitle it "A Successful College Student"

▸ Use plural here, because success requires more than just one quality.

to play ~~a role of a~~ *be* successful college student? A college ~~college~~ *university* student has more chances to get along with different people than *ever* before. ~~Due to the fact that~~ *Since* college time is a period that connects ~~the~~ *both* school life and social life, ~~what lie in front of them is that they need~~ *the student's primary goal is* to ~~prepared themselves~~ *himself* for stepping into the adult society~~;~~*.* ~~as a result~~ *Thus,* I think it is necessary for a successful college student to have two vital ~~ability~~ *abilities*: the ability to solve problems ~~he meets~~ and the ability to learn new knowledge.

Solving problems sounds simple, but actually it is not ~~an~~ *an* easy task. When we meet a problem, what should we do? Some people~~'s~~ *natural tendency* ~~will~~ *is to* flee from it ~~while~~*; however,* a successful ~~college student~~ *winner* should not do that. Indeed, he should face ~~it~~ *the difficulty squarely* and deal with ~~it~~ *the challenges* because he is no longer a neophyte who ~~first is~~ *is* ~~experiences~~ *experiencing* problems ~~for the first time.~~ ~~He~~ *A winner* should know how to handle *challenges* and make decisions while facing a problem since a

▸ The word "college" has appeared 5 times so far in the original; that is too much.

▸ Here one word replaces five.

▸ Note how you can use "life" once.

▸ Wow, this original sentence has 69 words! Way too many. Break it down.

▸ Avoid overusing "it."

college student is old enough to be his own master.

Secondly, ~~being~~ *as* a future member of ~~varied~~ *one of many* career fields, a successful college student must possess the ability to learn new knowledge *continually*. This *crucial* ability ~~would assist you to~~ *can help one* keep in touch with the ~~easy-to-change~~ *ever-changing* world. ~~In this~~ *today's* world, *where new technology is practically obsolete as soon as it hits the market shelves*, the information ~~is flashing~~ and knowledge ~~is often updating~~ *are always being updated*; hence, to survive and succeed ~~in this world~~, a college student must become familiar with new knowledge.

In conclusion, ~~in my opinion,~~ a successful college student should possess the ability *twin abilities* to solve problems and ~~the ability~~ to ~~learn~~ *acquire* new knowledge ~~both~~. ~~That would~~ *Possessing these skills will* distinguish you from a *the large* group of ordinary college students *and make you a winner—both in college and in life.*

> "Easy-to-change" is Chinglish.

> "World" has been used 3 times in this paragraph.

> If this paper is your opinion, you need not state this.

> "Learn" is okay, but it has been used already, and it is a weak verb.

> Note how the conclusion is now more powerful and enthusiastic...be a winner for life!

And here is the essay with the editing incorporated.   以下是修訂後的版本。

Draft 3

My Definition of a Successful College Student

What qualities does a successful college student need to possess? When one is admitted to college, what should he have if he wants to be successful? A university student has more chances to get along with different people than ever before. Since college is a period that connects both school and social life, the student's primary goal is to prepare himself for stepping into adult society. Thus, I think it is necessary for a successful college student to have two vital abilities: the ability to solve problems and the ability to learn new knowledge.

Solving problems sounds simple, but actually it is not an easy task. When we meet a problem, what should we do? Some people's natural tendency is to flee from it; however, a winner should not do that. Indeed, he should face the difficulty squarely and deal with the challenges because he is no longer a neophyte who is experiencing problems for the first time. A winner should know how to handle challenges and make decisions while facing a problem since a college student is old enough to be his own master.

Secondly, as a future member of one of many career fields, a successful college student must possess the ability to learn new knowledge continually. This crucial ability can help one keep in touch with the ever-changing world. In today's world, where new technology is practically obsolete as soon as it hits the market shelves, information and knowledge are always being updated; hence, to survive and succeed, a college student must become familiar with new knowledge.

In conclusion, a successful college student should possess the twin abilities to solve problems and to acquire new knowledge. Possessing these skills will distinguish you from the large group of ordinary college students and make you a winner—both in college and in life.

5 Comparison and Contrast
比較和對照

Long a favorite of writing teachers, the comparison and contrast essay looks at how two people, places, or things are both alike and different. This essay also requires careful organization to be clear to the reader. Below is one student's paper comparing and contrasting Taiwan and the U.S.

這是教寫作的老師向來所喜愛的文體，比較和對照性的文章是在檢視兩個人物、地方或事物間的異同之處，需要細心組織才能讓讀者清楚了解。以下的文章是同學所寫，比對台灣和美國的異同。

There are several different ways to organize such an essay. One method is point-by-point. In this style, the writer examines one point at a time, say, the lifestyles in Taiwan and the U.S., languages in both places, the economy of both, etc.

要組織這種文章有幾種不同的方式，其中一種是「重點比對」。這種方式是由作者一次檢視一個重點，例如台灣和美國的生活型態、兩地的語言、兩國的經濟等。

Point-by-Point Organization

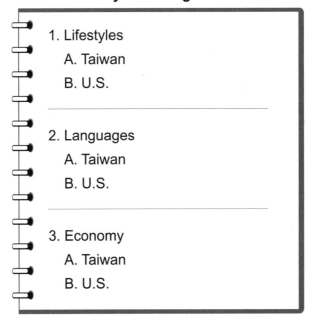

1. Lifestyles
   A. Taiwan
   B. U.S.

2. Languages
   A. Taiwan
   B. U.S.

3. Economy
   A. Taiwan
   B. U.S.

Another way to organize is the subject-by-subject approach. In this case, you may first examine the lifestyles, languages, and economy of Taiwan and then examine those same three items from the American point of view.

另一種方式是「主題比對」，你可以先檢視台灣的生活型態、語言和經濟之後，再從美國的觀點檢視相同的三個項目。

Subject-by-Subject Organization

1. Taiwan
    A. Lifestyles
    B. Languages
    C. Economy

2. U.S.
    A. Lifestyles
    B. Languages
    C. Economy

Now read the student's paper below. Does he or she use the point-by-point, or subject-by-subject approach, or something different?

現在閱讀以下這篇同學的作品，他／她是使用「重點比對」或「主題比對」？還是其他的方式？

Draft 1

Taiwan and The USA: Different but Alike

When we put Taiwan and America together, we might tell the differences between them with ease. For instance, they have different, or more accurately, opposite races; one is from the East while the other is derived from the West. Moreover, most Taiwanese believe in Buddhism and Taoism, going to temples to conjure, whereas over half of Americans are Christians. And, needless to say, people in two cultures use quite different languages; mandarin is often heard in Taiwan while English is understood all over the United State.

However, are there only differences we can find in these two opposite cultures? Actually no! If we give ourselves more times to have a second thought, then we might discover some likeness between them. Although the origins of people between Taiwan and the United States are exactly different, the structures of people are rather similar; that is, the two societies are both constructed of multiple races. For examples, there are ten sorts of aboriginals in Taiwan, and most of people have to speak Taiwanese if they want to communicate with southern people in Taiwan. And Americans, as we all know, are living in a land of immigrants. They have become accustomed to contacting many people from different cultures. Besides, another interesting point, people at both side appreciate each other's cultures. Americans admire Chinese cultures and Taiwanese admires American cultures. Americans like Chinese decorations, Chinese characters, Chinese martial art and so on. And we can find many American-style foods in Taiwan such as potato chips, hamburgers and hot dogs. Both peoples in Taiwan and the USA are devoted themselves to learning each other's languages.

Both peoples love to celebrate Christmas, and their building style in their modern cities are quite similar. Skyscrapers always confront the skyline in both Taiwan and the United States.

Here is the same essay, with editing.   以下是附上修訂的文章。

Draft 2

Taiwan and The USA: Different but _yet_ **Alike**

When we put _first contrast_ Taiwan and America together, we might tell the differences between them with ease. For instance, they have different, or more accurately, opposite races; one is from the East while the other is derived from the West. Moreover, most Taiwanese believe in Buddhism and Taoism, going to temples to conjure, whereas over half of Americans are Christians. And, needless to say, people in the two cultures use quite different languages; mandarin _Mandarin_ is ~~often heard~~ _widely spoken_ in Taiwan while English is understood all over the United States.

However, are there only differences we can find in these two opposite cultures? Actually no! If we give ourselves more times to ~~have a second thought~~ _think carefully_, then we might discover some likenesses between them. Although the origins of people ~~between~~ _in_ Taiwan and the United States are exactly different,

▸ For "USA," it is fine to just write "US".

▸ Add "s" to United States.

▸ "Second thoughts" is a common phrase, but it usually carries the idea of regret, such as, "She was going to marry Fred until she had second thoughts."

the structures of people are rather similar; that is, the two societies are both constructed of multiple races. For examples, there are ten ~~sorts of aboriginals~~ *ethnicities* in Taiwan, and most of people have to speak Taiwanese if they want to communicate with southern people in *Southern* Taiwan. And Americans, as we all know, are living in a land of immigrants. They have become accustomed to ~~contacting~~ *dealing with* many people from different cultures. Besides, another interesting point ~~is that,~~ people at *on* both sides appreciate each other's cultures. Americans admire Chinese cultures and Taiwanese admires American cultures. Americans like Chinese decorations, Chinese characters, Chinese martial arts and so on. And we can find many American-style foods in Taiwan such as potato chips, hamburgers and hot dogs. ~~Both~~ *Many* peoples in Taiwan and the USA are *now* devoted *devoting* themselves to learning each other's languages.

Both peoples love to celebrate Christmas, and their building styles in their modern cities are quite similar. Skyscrapers always ~~confront~~ *mark* the skyline in

> *"Confront" is the wrong word—it implies attacking.*

both Taiwan and the United States. While there are many obvious differences between Taiwan and the US, one may be surprised to find many similarities also...if one just takes the time to look for them!

> Note that this essay ended too suddenly; it needed a conclusion to wrap it up. For more on strong endings, please refer to "End with a Bang," Step 11, in Part C of this book.

Here is the essay, with editing built in.

以下是整合修訂後的文章。

Draft 3

Taiwan and The US: Different yet Alike

When we first contrast Taiwan and America, we might tell the differences between them with ease. For instance, they have different, or more accurately, opposite races; one is from the East while the other is derived from the West. Moreover, most Taiwanese believe in Buddhism and Taoism, going to temples to conjure, whereas over half of Americans are Christians. And, needless to say, people in the two cultures use quite different languages; Mandarin is widely spoken in Taiwan while English is understood all over the United States.

However, are there only differences we can find in these two opposite cultures? Actually no! If we give ourselves more time to think carefully, then we might discover some likenesses between them. Although the origins of people in Taiwan and the United States are different, the structures of people are rather similar; that is, the two societies are both constructed of multiple races. For example, there are ten aboriginal ethnicities in Taiwan, and most people have to speak Taiwanese if they want to communicate with people in Southern Taiwan. And Americans, as we all know, are living in a land of immigrants. They have become accustomed to dealing with many people from different cultures. Besides, another interesting point is that people on both sides appreciate each other's cultures. Americans admire Chinese culture and Taiwanese admire American culture. Americans like Chinese decorations, Chinese characters, Chinese martial arts and so on. And we can find many American-style foods in Taiwan such as potato chips, hamburgers and hot dogs. Many people in Taiwan and the US are now devoting themselves to learning each other's languages.

Both peoples love to celebrate Christmas, and their building styles in their modern cities are quite similar. Skyscrapers always mark the skyline in both Taiwan and the United States. While there are many obvious differences between Taiwan and the US, one may be surprised to find many similarities also...if one just takes the time to look for them!

Did you notice the author's style? Rather than using a point-by-point or subject-by-subject approach, the writer examined the differences first, followed by the similarities, and the title shows this organization clearly.

你注意到作者的風格了嗎？作者並未使用「重點比對」或「主題比對」，而是先檢視不同的地方，接著是相同之處，而且題目已經清楚顯示出這種組織方式了。

Before we go on, here are a few key words or phrases to help you with your Comparison and Contrast Essay. Use a variety of these words and phrases; do not overuse just one or two. These are "direction words" that help the reader follow the ideas that are similar or different.

在我們往下看之前，有幾個重要字彙或片語可以幫助你撰寫比較和對照的文體。多使用這些不同的字彙或片語，而不要過度使用其中的一兩個字。這些是所謂的「方向字」，有助於讀者理解意見的異同。

Ways to Express SIMILARITIES (Comparison)	Ways to Express DIFFERENCES (Contrast)
• alike • also • same • too • as well • as well as • in the same way • in addition to • similarly	• however • but • yet • different • in contrast • on the other hand

6 Cause and Effect
因果關係

This paper looks at *why* certain things happen (cause) and the *results* that happen afterward (effect). When you think about it, most things in life have a Cause and Effect relationship, whether good or bad. If you speak kindly to people, they are generally kind to you. If you work hard on a paper, you tend to get a better grade. If you are rude to others, they tend to be rude to you. This is all summed up in an old English saying that comes from the Bible: "You reap what you sow." The Chinese have a similar saying: "種瓜得瓜，種豆得豆。" (Simply put, you get out of life what you put into it, and the fact that you have read this far into this book shows me you will reap a benefit because you have invested time and energy into it.)

這種文章表達為何某些事情會發生（因）以及發生之後的結果（果）。其實仔細想一下，生活中大部分的事情不論是好是壞都有因果關係。如果你對人講話和善，他們通常也會和善待你。如果你認真寫作，通常會得到較好的成績。如果你對他人粗魯，他們也會對你還以顏色。這些都可以用聖經中的一句傳統英文諺語來概括：「人種的是什麼，收的也是什麼。」中國也有類似的諺語：「種瓜得瓜，種豆得豆。」（簡單來說，你種下什麼因，就收何種果。你已經讀了本書這麼多篇幅，因為你所投入的閱讀時間和精力，我相信你也會獲益良多。）

Here is a student's Cause and Effect outline and essay about a huge health crisis facing both Taiwan and especially the U.S.: obesity.

以下是同學的一篇因果關係文章的大綱以及本文，題目是有關台灣以及特別是美國所面臨的健康危機：肥胖。

Outline 1

I. Introduction
   1. Bring out obesity

II. Cause and effect of obesity
   1. Overeating causes obesity.
   2. Lack of exercise leads to obesity.
   3. Obesity results in other diseases.
   4. Obesity also relates to discrimination.

III. Conclusion
   1. People should be careful of obesity.

Draft 1

Know More about Obesity

People are getting more and more hatred toward obesity. It is an invisible killer that does harm people. Obesity is also noticed by everyone from all over the world, even governments nowadays. People pay attention to it, worrying it will take one's life away. In general, overeating is the main reason that causes obesity, followed by lack of exercise. Obesity also has a great influence on one's health. Thus, people should know more about obesity for one's own good.

Eating a lot, overeating, will result in obesity. People get energy they need for daily lives from the food they have. Generally speaking, people do not need too much food to maintain their need. The calories a grownup needs are 2200 to 3000 calories. However, due to the high living standards, people enjoy a lot and eat much more than before. They then absorb more calories. If the calories one takes exceed that one consumes, those calories may be stored in one's body as fat. People then become heavier and heavier. About 39% of obese people eat too much than they are supposed to eat, according to a survey of Department of Health. In addition, people who have lots of deep-fried food as their meals most of the time are more likely to be diagnosed as obesity since they intake more fat from deep-fried food. In news reported in America, nutritionists in America are working hard to solve the problem of obesity in the U.S. Those nutritionists think the old eating habit should be changed. Old eating style says people should eat high-carbohydrate food to get more calories because people in old days needed more calories to work. Nevertheless, nutritionists nowadays indicate people should have low-carbohydrate food to reduce calories. It may help people who eat too much to get away from obesity.

Another reason that will lead to obesity is lack of exercise. If one does not do exercise regularly to consume his/her extra calories, he/she is likely to put on weight, and has the possibility to suffer from obesity. This kind of situation is apt to happen to modern people who live bustling lives in order to earn as much money as they can, such as the blue-collared and the white-collared. They feel exhausted after the long weekdays; as a result, they are not willing to go out on weekends. Staying home and no exercise are responsible for gaining weight. On the other hand, children also have the problem of obesity. According to a survey, nearly 24% of all children are overweight. This number can be attributed to the lack of exercise. Nowadays, most children are addicted to computer games or TV programs. They are so called mouse potatoes or couch potatoes. They stay at home most of the time, and they eat lots of junk food while enjoying their entertainment. Their lack of exercise and disordered eating contribute to their obesity. Government in Taiwan advocates the "exercise 333 principles," that is, do exercise three times a week, at least thirty minutes a time, and the rate of heartbeat per minute should reach 130. It is evident that people can stay healthy if they follow the principle according to a research.

One's health condition is tightly related to obesity. Excessive body weight has been shown to predispose to considerable diseases such as cardiovascular diseases, diabetes, and high blood pressure. In a study, researchers carry out several experiments and find that obesity causes disordered fat in blood, leading to the rising of cholesterol, low-density cholesterol, and triglyceride. The rising will lead to the falling of high-density cholesterol that protects cardiovascular system. As for diabetes, fatness restrains the secretion of insulin. If the insulin in blood reduces, the dextrose in blood increases, and people then have the possibility to be diagnosed as diabetes. When it comes to high blood pressure, obesity is much more related to it. Much cholesterol combines with fat to become lipoprotein, which permeates into the wall of blood vessel with the circulation of blood. Lipoprotein gathers in blood, narrows the blood vessels, and causes atherosclerosis. Because of atherosclerosis, blood pressure rises, and high blood pressure happens. American research indicates that more than one third of high blood pressure patients are obese.

Obesity has become a great issue in the world since more and more people suffer from obesity and even die of its related diseases. It seems to be not important but plays an influential role for everyone, especially on one's life. According to statistic, forty per cent of obese people live less longer than those who are thin. The life expectancy of obese people is only half of ordinary people. Governments around the world try to find solutions for obesity. They are eager to reduce the number of obese people. Whatever the policies are, it is people themselves who should be responsible for their health.

Now here is the essay, with editing.　　　　　　　　　以下是附有修訂的文章。

Outline 2

I. Introduction

　　1. A. Bring out Define obesity

　　B. Show the dangers of obesity

→ A category needs at least two sub-points.

II. Causes and effects of obesity

　　1. A. Overeating causes obesity.

2. B. Lack of exercise leads to obesity.

3. C. Obesity results in other diseases.

4. D. Obesity also relates to discrimination.

> You need at least TWO sub-points for each category. Also, use Roman numerals (I, II, III) for the main points, capital letters (A, B, C) for the next sub-points, then Arabic numerals (1, 2, 3) for the next sub-points.

III. Conclusion

1. A. People should be careful of obesity.

B. People should take responsibility for their own health and weight.

Draft 2

Know More about Obesity

> In this case, one word is enough.

People are getting more and more hatred toward concerned about obesity. It is an invisible a silent killer that does greatly harms people. Obesity is also noticed by everyone garnering attention from all over the world, even from governments nowadays. People pay attention to it, worrying if it will take one's life away. In general, overeating is the main reason that causes of obesity, followed by lack of exercise. Obesity also has a great influence on one's health. Thus, people should know more about obesity for one's their own good.

> "Hatred" is too strong.

> It is not invisible.

> refers to antecedent, "people"

~~Eating a lot,~~ *Serious* overeating, ~~will result in~~ *often* *causes* obesity. ~~People~~ *We* get *the* energy ~~they~~ *we* need for *our* daily lives from the food ~~they have~~. Generally speaking, ~~people~~ *we* do not need too much food to maintain *our energy level and meet* ~~their~~ *our* needs. ~~The calories a grownup~~ *An average adult* needs are *only* 2,200 to 3,000 calories *a day*. However, due to ~~the~~ *our wealth and* high living standards, people *today* ~~enjoy a lot and~~ eat much more than *ever* before. They then absorb more calories. If the calories ~~one takes~~ *people consume* exceed ~~that one consumes~~ *those burned up,* those calories may be stored ~~in one's~~ body as fat. People then become heavier and heavier. About 39% of obese people eat ~~too much~~ *more* than they are supposed to eat, according to a survey of *the* *R.O.C.* Department of Health. In addition, people who have *consume* ~~lots of~~ *many* deep-fried foods ~~as their meals most of the time~~ are more likely to be diagnosed as ~~obesity~~ *obese* since they ~~intake more fat from deep-fried foods~~ *are loaded with fat and calories*. In news reported in America, nutritionists ~~in America~~ *there* are working hard to solve the problem of obesity ~~in the U.S.~~.

> "Grownup" sounds like what a child would call an adult.

> Define your source.

> "Lots of" is informal language, better for speaking but not for writing.

> Redundant.

> "Obese" is the adjective.

Those nutritionists think the old eating habits should be changed. ~~Old~~ The old eating style says people should eat high-carbohydrate foods to get more calories because people in ~~old~~ days the past needed more calories to ~~work~~ do physical labor. Nevertheless, most nutritionists nowadays indicate people should have low-carbohydrate food diets to reduce calories. ~~It~~ Such a change may help people who ~~eat too much~~ overeat to ~~get away from~~ avoid obesity.

→ four words replaced by one

Another reason ~~that will lead to~~ cause of obesity is lack of exercise. If one does not do exercise regularly to consume ~~his/her~~ extra calories, he/she is likely to gradually put on weight~~,~~ and ~~has the possibility to~~ may later suffer from obesity. This kind of situation is apt to happen to modern people, whether blue- or white-collar, who live bustling lives in order to earn as much money as they can~~, such as the blue-collared and the white-collared~~. They feel exhausted after the long weekdays; as a result, they are not willing to go out on weekends. Staying home ~~and no~~ without exercise ~~are responsible for~~ can cause one to gaining weight.

→ five words replaced by two

→ use "exercise" as a verb, and cut "do."

~~On the other hand~~ *In addition,* *many* children also ~~have the problem of~~ *suffer from* obesity. According to ~~a~~ *one* survey, nearly 24% of all children are overweight. This number can be attributed to the lack of exercise. ~~Nowadays~~ *Today,* ~~most~~ *many* children are addicted to computer games or TV programs. ~~They are~~ *These* so-called mouse potatoes or couch potatoes~~.~~ They stay at home ~~most~~ *much* of the time, ~~and they~~ eat*ing* lots of junk food while enjoying their entertainment. ~~Their~~ *Such a* lack of exercise and ~~disordered~~ *poor* eating habits *easily* contribute to their obesity. ~~Government~~ *The government* in Taiwan advocates the "~~exercise~~ *Exercise* 333 ~~principle~~ *Principle*," that is, do exercise three times a week, at least thirty minutes a time, and ~~the rate of heartbeat per minute~~ should reach 130 *beats per minute.* ~~It is evident that people can~~ *Clearly there is a strong link between* stay*ing* healthy ~~if they~~ *and* follow*ing* the *333* ~~principle~~ *Principle* ~~according to a research.~~

One's health ~~condition~~ is ~~tightly~~ *closely* related to obesity. Excessive body weight has been shown to

▶ I suggest a new paragraph here.

▶ The author needs to say if this is in the U.S., Taiwan, or where.

▶ "Most" involves an assumption that is not really provable. Avoid assumptions and focus on provable facts.

predispose *one* to considerable diseases such as cardiovascular diseases, diabetes, and high blood pressure. In a *one* study, researchers ~~carry~~ *carried* out several experiments and ~~find~~ *found* that obesity causes disordered fat in blood, leading to ~~the~~ *a* ~~rising~~ *rise* of cholesterol, low-density cholesterol, and triglycerides. ~~The rising will~~ *This rise may* lead to the ~~falling~~ of high-density (*so-called "good"*) cholesterol that protects ~~the~~ cardiovascular system. As for diabetes, fatness restrains the secretion of insulin. If the insulin in blood ~~reduces~~ *is reduced*, the dextrose in ~~the~~ blood increases, and people ~~then have the possibility to be diagnosed as~~ *are more likely to get* diabetes. When it comes to high blood pressure, obesity is ~~much more~~ *closely* related ~~to it~~ *as well*. Much cholesterol combines with fat to become lipoprotein, which permeates into the wall of ~~the~~ blood vessel with the circulation of blood. Lipoprotein gathers in blood, narrows the blood vessels, and causes atherosclerosis. Because of atherosclerosis, blood pressure rises, and high blood pressure ~~happens~~ *results*. American research indicates that more than

> *Be careful with "will." Few things in this world are 100%. Words like "may" are usually safer to use.*

one third of high blood pressure patients are obese.

Obesity has become a great issue in the world since more and more people suffer from obesity and even die of ~~from~~ its related diseases. It *may* seems ~~to be not~~ *un*important but ~~plays an influential role for everyone,~~ ~~especially on one's life~~ *it actually is a large threat.* According to *one* statistic, forty per cent of obese people live ~~less longer~~ *shorter lives* than those who are thin. The life expectancy of obese people is only half *that* of ordinary people. Governments around the world *are* try*ing* to find solutions for obesity. They are eager to reduce the number of obese people. Whatever the policies are, it is people themselves who should be responsible for their health.

> The author needs to cite his/her source for each study.

Here is the outline and essay with corrections included.

以下是修訂完後的大綱和本文。

Outline 3

I. Introduction
　　A. Define obesity
　　B. Show the dangers of obesity

II. Causes and effects of obesity

    A. Overeating causes obesity.

    B. Lack of exercise leads to obesity.

    C. Obesity results in other diseases.

    D. Obesity also relates to discrimination.

III. Conclusion

    A. People should be careful of obesity.

    B. People should take responsibility for their own health and weight.

Draft 3

Obesity

People are getting more and more concerned about obesity. It is a silent killer that greatly harms people. Obesity is also garnering attention from all over the world, even from governments nowadays. People pay attention to it, worrying if it will take one's life away. In general, overeating is the main cause of obesity, followed by lack of exercise. Obesity also has a great influence on one's health. Thus, people should know more about obesity for their own good.

Serious overeating often causes obesity. We get the energy we need for our daily lives from food. Generally speaking, we do not need too much food to maintain our energy level and meet our needs. An average adult needs only 2,200 to 3,000 calories a day. However, due to our wealth and high living standards, people today eat much more than ever before. They then absorb more calories. If the calories people consume exceed those burned up, those calories may be stored as fat.

People then become heavier and heavier. About 39% of obese people eat more than they are supposed to eat, according to a survey of the R.O.C. Department of Health. In addition, people who consume many deep-fried foods are more likely to be diagnosed as obese since deep-fried foods are loaded with fat and calories. In news reported in America, nutritionists there are working hard to solve the problem of obesity. Those nutritionists think the old eating habits should be changed. The old eating style says people should eat high-carbohydrate foods to get more calories because people in the past needed more calories to do physical labor. Nevertheless, most nutritionists nowadays indicate people should have low-carbohydrate diets to reduce calories. Such a change may help people who overeat avoid obesity.

Another cause of obesity is lack of exercise. If one does not exercise regularly to consume extra calories, he is likely to gradually put on weight and may later suffer from obesity. This kind of situation is apt to happen to modern people, whether blue- or white-collar, who live bustling lives in order to earn as much money as they can. They feel exhausted after the long weekdays; as a result, they are not willing to go out on weekends. Staying home without exercise can cause one to gain weight.

In addition, many children suffer from obesity. According to one survey, nearly 24% of all children are overweight. This number can be attributed to the lack of exercise. Today, many children are addicted to computer games or TV programs. These so-called mouse potatoes or couch potatoes stay at home much of the time, eating lots of junk food while enjoying their entertainment. Such a lack of exercise and poor eating habits easily contribute to obesity. The government in Taiwan advocates the "Exercise 333 Principle," that is, exercise three times a week, at least thirty minutes a time, and the heartbeat should reach 130 beats per minute. Clearly there is a strong link between staying healthy and following the 333 Principle.

One's health is closely related to obesity. Excessive body weight has been shown to predispose one to considerable diseases such as cardiovascular diseases, diabetes, and high blood pressure. In one study, researchers carried out several experiments and found that obesity causes disordered fat in blood, leading to a rise of cholesterol, low-density cholesterol, and triglycerides. This rise may lead to the fall of high-density (so-called "good") cholesterol that protects the cardiovascular system. As for diabetes, fatness restrains the secretion of insulin. If the insulin in blood is reduced, dextrose in the blood increases, and people are more likely to get diabetes. When it comes to high blood pressure, obesity is closely related as well. Much cholesterol combines with fat to become lipoprotein, which permeates into the wall of the blood vessel with the circulation of blood. Lipoprotein gathers in blood, narrows the blood vessels, and causes atherosclerosis. Because of atherosclerosis, blood pressure rises, and high blood pressure results. American research indicates that more than one third of high blood pressure patients are obese.

Obesity has become a great issue in the world since more and more people suffer from obesity and even die from its related diseases. It may seem unimportant but it actually is a large threat. According to one statistic, forty per cent of obese people live shorter lives than those who are thin. The life expectancy of obese people is only half that of ordinary people. Governments around the world are trying to find solutions for obesity. They are eager to reduce the number of obese people. Whatever the policies are, it is people themselves who should be responsible for their health.

7 Persuasive
說服性

My personal favorite, the persuasive paper simply tries to get the reader to do something, whether it is buy product A or vote for candidate X. You have been doing this since you were a child. Think about when you tried to get your parents to buy something for you or let you stay up later one night.

這是我個人最喜歡的文類，說服性文章企圖說服讀者去做某事，例如去購買某產品或投票給某候選人。你從童年時期就開始說服別人，回想一下你以前如何說服爸媽掏腰包買東西給你，或是允許你晚上可以晚點上床睡覺。

One common place for you to use this writing style is the dreaded <u>college application</u>. You need to persuade someone, someone whose desk is already FULL of papers, that YOU are the one he or she should let in! How do you do it? Be persuasive!

一個常要使用這種寫作文體的情況就是令人心驚膽顫的大學申請書。你要說服一個桌上早已堆滿申請書的人，你才是具備資格的人選。那你應該如何寫呢？就是要有說服力！

Below is a college essay from a Taiwanese student who had studied in the U.S. for a few years during high school, making her case why the college should let her in.

以下是一名在美國高中讀過幾年書的台灣大學生所寫的文章，她要說服學校讓她入學。

Draft 1

As an international student attending an international school, I have met and befriended many people from different countries: Korea, Japan, Pakistan, China, and of course the U.S. I always like to have many friends from different countries and learn their different cultures; for example, I have even learned from my Korean friends how to say and write some Korean. Attending the international school and having numerous friends from different countries has provided me with a better, deeper, richer view of the world.

With honor and gratitude, this year I became the vice-president of the senior class. From my point of view, being a vice-president is not only a title or responsibility, but also an acknowledgment of my leadership and social relationships with other students. In addition, I have gained the award of House Mom's "dream girl." I feel this demonstrates my successful relationships with adults, too. I have also joined the dance troupe at the school. In my opinion, dancing not only helps build a stronger physique, but also improves social relationships. I really like to social with other people.

My study in Taiwan also gives me a strong foundation of knowledge; it contribute to my recent good academic performance. I had been hard working during my school year in Taiwan and have good relationship with my teachers and all my classmates. I had been secretary for two years in my high school in Taiwan.

Now, in the United State, I am in AP calculus and AP statistic class. I try to take pre-college courses as many as I can, and also challenge myself as much as I can in life. In addition, I have been in my high school's honor group since the first year I came here until now. It acknowledges and demonstrates my consistency in hard working and my diligent study.

If given the honor of studying at University of Nebraska[3], I believe my international experiences, my social relationship, and my hard working make me unique.

---

3 The name has been changed.

Here is the paper with revisions added.   以下是加入修訂的文章。

Draft 2

As an international student *now* attending an international *boarding* school, I have met and befriended many people from different countries: Korea, Japan, Pakistan, China, and of course the U.S. I always like to have many friends from different countries and learn their different cultures; for example, I have even learned from my Korean friends how to say and write some Korean. Attending the international school and having numerous friends from different countries has provided me with a better, deeper, richer view of the world.

With *feelings of* honor and gratitude, this year I became the vice-president of the senior class. From my point of view, being a vice-president is *was* not only a title or responsibility, but also an acknowledgment of my leadership and social relationships with other students. In addition, I have ~~gained~~ *earned* the award ~~of~~ House Mom's "~~dream girl~~ *Dream Girl*" award. *Though some may think it silly,* I feel this *honor* demonstrates

→ *Keep a consistent past tense in this paragraph.*

demonstrated my successful relationships with adults, too. I have also joined the dance troupe at the school. In my opinion, dancing not only helps build a stronger physique, but also improves social relationships. We humans are "social creatures," and that is definitely true in my case. I really like to greatly enjoy social interactions with other people.

My earlier academic study studies in Taiwan also gives gave me a strong foundation of knowledge; it those years contributed to my recent good academic performance. I had been hard working worked hard during my school year while in Taiwan and have had good relationships with my teachers and all my classmates. For two years I had been served as class secretary for two years in my high school in Taiwan.

Now, in the United States, I am in AP calculus and AP statistics classes. I try have tried to take pre-college as many college-prep courses as many as I can possible, both to enhance my learning and also because I like to challenge myself as much as I can in life. In addition,

I have been in my high school's *academic* honor group ~~society~~ since the first year I came here until now. ~~It acknowledges and demonstrates~~ *This distinction shows* my ~~consistency in hard working~~ *consistent work ethic* and my diligent study *habits*.

If given the honor of studying at *the* University of Nebraska, I believe my international experiences, my *healthy* social relationships, and ~~my hard working~~ *strong work ethic will* make me *a* unique *and valuable member of your community*.

Here is the persuasive paper with the revisions built in. 以下是修訂完後的說服性文章。

Draft 3

As an international student now attending an international boarding school, I have met and befriended many people from different countries: Korea, Japan, Pakistan, China, and of course the U.S. I always like to have many friends from different countries and learn their different cultures; for example, I have even learned from my Korean friends how to say and write some Korean. Attending the international school and having numerous friends from different countries has provided me with a better, deeper, richer view of the world.

With feelings of honor and gratitude, this year I became the vice-president of the senior class. From my point of view, being a vice-president was not only a title or responsibility, but also an acknowledgment of my leadership and social relationships with other students. In addition, I earned the House Mom's "Dream Girl" award. Though some may think it silly, I feel this honor demonstrated my successful relationships with adults, too. I also joined the dance troupe at the school. In my opinion, dancing not only helps build a stronger physique, but also improves social relationships. We humans are "social creatures," and that is definitely true in my case. I greatly enjoy social interactions with other people.

My earlier academic studies in Taiwan also gave me a strong foundation of knowledge; those years contributed to my recent good academic performance. I worked hard while in Taiwan and had good relationships with my teachers and classmates. For two years I served as class secretary in my high school in Taiwan.

Now, in the United States, I am in AP calculus and AP statistics classes. I have tried to take as many college-prep courses as possible, both to enhance my learning and also because I like to challenge myself as much as I can in life. In addition, I have been in my high school's academic honor society since the first year I came here until now. This distinction shows my consistent work ethic and diligent study habits.

If given the honor of studying at the University of Nebraska, I believe my international experiences, healthy social relationships, and strong work ethic will make me a unique and valuable member of your community.

Gentle Reader, I know this section with several essays has been long, but I hope you have gained some practical help by seeing several different kinds of writing tasks and how they can be improved. Below, the next sections will give you specific tips to sharpen your writing.

親愛的讀者，我知道以上這章因附上幾篇文章而顯得比較長，但我希望你能從不同文類的寫作以及如何改進當中獲得一些實質的協助。下一章會提供你具體的寫作訣竅來增進你的寫作能力。

Part B

Some Key Usage Points— Avoid Chinglish

精要關鍵用字── 避免中式英文

Some Key Usage Points
—Avoid Chinglish

精要關鍵用字——避免中式英文

Please let me be honest. There is no way I can list each grammar and word choice point you may need when you write in English. That would require a separate and very thick book. But the good news is, I do not *need* to, because other books have *already been written* that do a fine job of explaining English grammar. One example is *Grammar in Use: Reference and Practice for Intermediate Students of English* (3rd edition), by Raymond Murphy (Cambridge University Press: 2004.) What I *do* wish to do in this section is to share with you a few common problems I have seen from Chinese speakers who write in English. Learn these tips and you will see your writing skills improve. As my wonderful French professor at William and Mary, Dr. Clare Mather, used to say: "You think you're making hundreds of mistakes, but you're actually just making about 20 mistakes hundreds of times. Correct those few mistakes, and you'll see your French get a lot better." The same is true of your English.

What is Chinglish? It is Chinese-English. It is perfectly normal, when you learn a foreign language, that you *think* in your native tongue and try to translate word-for-word. Though this is a normal, understandable trait, it makes your foreign language sound, well,

我還是誠實一點，我是不可能把你在英文寫作時所需的所有文法和用字都列出來，那需要一本非常厚重的書才能辦得到。但好消息是我不需要去做這件事，因為市面上已經有其他解釋詳盡的英文文法書，例如 Raymond Murphy 所編著的《Grammar in Use: Reference and Practice for Intermediate Students of English》（第三版）（劍橋大學出版社，2004）。在本章我將點出華人在英文寫作時的一些常見問題，學習這些要點可以改善你的寫作。我以前在 William and Mary 學院的法文教授 Clare Mather 博士常說：「你以為你犯了數百個錯誤，其實你只是犯了約 20 個錯誤數百次。只要改正那些少數的錯誤，你就會發現你的法文突飛猛進。」這些話也適用在英文學習上。

什麼是 Chinglish ？就是中式英文。學習外語時用母語思考並逐字翻譯，這是很正常的現象。然而，雖然這種現象很正常且合理，但它就是會讓你的外文聽起來不道地。舉例來說，我初學中文時學到 old 的中文意

foreign. For instance, when I was first learning Chinese, I learned the word for old was *lao*（老）. When it came time to talk about old clothes, though, my friend corrected me and said I had to say *jiu*（舊）. I was puzzled because English has the same word for old dog or old clothes: old. It took me time to think in Chinese, and it also takes Chinese speakers time to *think* in English. But be encouraged! Learning English just takes time and patience.

Surely you too know many funny examples of Chinglish, where people get the two languages confused, but here is one more story before we go on. For two years I taught an English writing class at Tsing Hua University; I was impressed with the students' abilities and diligence. One student, Lisa, particularly impressed me as a strong writer; her papers were always clear and interesting. But one day I was reading along, all clear, when she made a reference to "sweet grass." *Sweet grass*? What did she mean? I reread the passage, looking for context clues, but still had no idea what she meant. Then the thought entered my mind: is she referring to *marijuana*? Lisa?! The next time we had class, I asked her about it. "Lisa, this is a great paper, but I just have one question: what is "sweet grass?" She smiled and told me the Chinese name, *xiang cao*（香草）: vanilla!

Be aware of these common Chinglish errors. They may not be exactly wrong grammatically, but they sound odd to native speakers of English. And not all the items

思是「老」，但當我用來表達「老衣服」時，我的朋友卻糾正我說用要「舊」這個字。這讓我很困惑，因為英文可以用 old 來表示 old dog 或 old clothes。我花了不少時間才有辦法用中文思考，同樣地，華人也需要一段時間才能學會用英文思考。但是不要沮喪，學習英文只是需要時間和耐心。

你應該也知道許多中式英文的有趣例子，很多人會混淆這兩種語言。在往下看之前，我再說一個故事。我曾在清華大學教過兩年英文寫作，我很欣賞那些學生的能力和用功。其中一名學生 Lisa 的表現相當好，文章總是非常清楚有趣，讓我印象特別深刻。有一天我在看她的作文，大部分寫得都還不錯，但有個地方她提到 sweet grass，我覺得很納悶，這是什麼意思？我再重讀一遍，想從前後文找出線索，但仍然不知所云。我無來由地想，難道她指的是大麻？Lisa ？！下一次上課時我就問她：「Lisa，這篇作文寫得很好，只是我有個問題，sweet grass 是什麼意思啊？」Lisa 笑著回答說就是中文的香草，喔，原來是英文的 vanilla ！

要注意這些常見的中式英文，它們的文法或許沒有錯，但對英語母語人士而言，卻是很奇怪的用法。以下的用字說明並不都是針對中式英文，

in this section are Chinglish. Some are just tricky rules that many native speakers of English have a hard time with too! Also, some are idioms that simply do not translate directly.

有些麻煩的用法連英語母語人士也會搞錯，另外有些片語是無法直接翻譯的。

1 Afraid
害怕

This is a very common phrase, （我很怕蚊子）. But be careful: in English, "afraid" means actual fear, so do not say, "I am afraid of mosquitoes." That gives the image of some 200-pound mosquito trying to kill you! In this case, just write: "I hate mosquitoes" or "I find mosquitoes annoying." Save "afraid" for serious cases.

「我很怕蚊子」是中文裡常見的說法，但要小心，在英文中 afraid 是指真正的懼怕，所以不能說 I am afraid of mosquitoes.，那會讓人誤以為有隻 200 磅的蚊子要攻擊你！這句話只要寫成 I hate mosquitoes. 或 I find mosquitoes annoying. 就可以了，把 afraid 用在更嚴重的情況吧。

- Ever since I was bitten as a child, I have always been afraid of big dogs.
- With the economy doing poorly, I am afraid I may have a hard time finding a job.

2 Bored/Boring
無聊

These adjectives that can end with either -ed or -ing can be tricky. In general, *bored* is how someone feels because a situation (or another person) is *boring*.

這類用 -ed 或 -ing 結尾的形容詞很容易讓人搞錯。一般而言，bored 指的是某人的感受，因為他所處的情境（或面對的人）很 boring。

- ✘ This class is too long. I feel very **boring**.
- ✔ This class is too long. I feel very bored.

To say *you* are boring is to insult yourself! But a boring class can make a person bored.

如果你說自己很 boring，那就等於在侮辱自己了。但是你可以說一堂 boring class 讓人感到 bored。

There are quite a few of these -ing and -ed adjective pairs:

以下有幾組 -ing 和 -ed 並列的形容詞：

amazing — amazed	embarrassing — embarrassed
confusing — confused	exciting — excited
depressing — depressed	interesting — interested
disgusting — disgusted	shocking — shocked

Although you would normally not use both words of the same pair so close together, here are a few examples to let you get the hang of it.

雖然你通常不會在鄰近的句子中同時使用以上同一組的兩個字，但以下的例句可以讓你很快就學會它們的用法。

- That was an amazing concert! I was amazed by the musicians' skill!

- This movie is so depressing. I feel absolutely depressed!

- Mom told my boyfriend an embarrassing story from my childhood; I felt so embarrassed!

▪ **Activity**

2.1 Now you try it: Fill in the blank with the best word from the chart on the previous page to complete each sentence.

現在換你來練習看看：在空格內填入上頁表格中的適當單字，使整句的句意完整。

1. John Steinbeck's novel *The Grapes of Wrath* is so d_____; it is about a family struggling during the Great Depression of the 1930s, and they kept failing over and over.

2. *Argh*, this class is so b_____! I keep staring at the clock, waiting for it to be over!

3. I have been sitting here for two hours, waiting for them to fix my car. I did not bring anything to read or do. I feel b_____ to tears!

4. Hey, you should read this book about WW II: it has some a_____ stories in it!

5. Do you dare tell me about your most e_____ moment?

6. Smoking really is a d_____ habit; try to stay away from cigarettes.

7. If you do not read Chinese, trying to figure out street signs in Taiwan can be very c_____.

8. "Ever since my girlfriend started going with another guy, I have felt so d_____," Sam sighed.

9. I felt so e_____ when the teacher said I had gotten the lowest grade in the class.

10. The fact that you have read this far in this book shows how i_____ you are in improving your English writing. *Bravo*!

(Answers are in the Answer Key on page 196.)

3 Colors
顏色

This is an easy problem to solve. Because the Chinese word for *white* is *bai se*（白色）, many translate it as "white color," as in "Have you seen my dog? It is white color." No. All you need to say is "Have you seen my dog? It is white."

這個問題比較容易解決。中文稱 white 為「白色」，因此很多人會把中文的「白色」翻譯成 white color，例如：Have you seen my dog? It is white color. 這是不對的，你只要說 Have you seen my dog? It is white. 就可以了。

✗ **Blue color** makes me feel peaceful.

✔ Blue makes me feel peaceful.

✗ **Red color and yellow color** can make people feel in a hurry.

✔ Red and yellow can make people feel in a hurry.

(And what are the main colors at McDonald's? Red and yellow. That's why they call it "fast food." They want you to spend your money and get out fast so they have room for the next person.)

（麥當勞的主要顏色為何？紅黃兩色！因此它們又被稱為「速食」。他們希望消費者付錢之後就馬上離開，這樣他們才能服務下一名顧客。）

4 Easy to
易於

This is a common expression in Chinese, but when directly translated to English, it becomes Chinglish. Below are some simple ways to express this idea in English.

這是中文常見的用語，但是若直接譯成英文就會變成中式英文。以下是用英文表達「易於…」的簡單方式。

Chinglish	Much Better
• easy to angry	• get angry easily • bad-tempered
• easy to break	• breakable • break easily • fragile—handle with care
• easy to change	• ever-changing • easily changeable
• easy to irritate	• easily irritated • irritable

Examples of proper usage:　　　　　　　　　適當用法的例句如下：

- This glass breaks easily, so please put a "Fragile—Handle with Care" sticker on the box before you mail it.

- We live in an ever-changing world, so we must always be flexible and willing to learn new skills.

- "My Dad gets angry really easily," Jack said, "so I don't like to spend much time at home."

- Without enough sleep, it is easy to feel very irritable.

5 Ever
曾經

This is a fine English word, used for past tense, but it is normally used in questions only!

這是個很好的英文字，通常用於過去式，而且只用在問句中。

- I have ever been to California. (**Chinglish**)

Instead, use "ever" + past participle in questions and "before" in statements.

要表達「曾經…」的概念時，在問句時要用「ever + 過去分詞」，在陳述句時要用 before。例如：

- Have you ever been to California?
- Have you ever been very depressed?
- Have you ever taken swimming lessons?

Here are some ways to express past tense in statements. Note the use of "before."

以下是在陳述句中表達過去時態，注意 before 的用法。

- I have been to California before.
- I have been depressed before.
- I have taken swimming lessons before.

6 He or She (or It?)
他、她、它

You know this one, but slow down and make sure you are right. Here again Chinese is wonderfully simple: just say *ta*（他／她）, and all is well. But this is a big deal in English; get it wrong and you will confuse people, or sound silly, or both. I know many people with *excellent* English who still get this wrong sometimes. Just be careful.

你早就知道它們的用法了，但是稍等一下，先確認你是否用對了。中文的用法很簡單，說「ㄊㄚ」時可以代表他或她。但是在英文裡卻是個大問題，用錯了就讓人摸不著頭緒。我認識很多英文很棒的人，有時仍會用錯這些字，所以還是小心至上。

- ✗ My father is 60 years old. **She** is a nice person.
- ✗ I miss my mother, but **he** is coming to visit me at New Year's.

Always use *he* or *him* with males, and *she* or *her* with females.

指涉男性只能用 he 或 him，而女性只能用 she 或 her。

What about *it*? Simple: use *it* with things that have no gender, like non-living things, or animals where you are unsure of the gender.

那 it 怎麼使用呢？很簡單，用在沒有性別之分的事物，如沒有生命的東西，或你不確定性別的動物上。

- It is a beautiful house, but it is out of our price range. Sorry.

- That dog is so mean; I wish the police would take it away!

If you know the animal's gender, go ahead and say *he* or *she*.

如果你知道該動物的性別，那就使用 he 或 she。

- We sure miss Little Yellow; she was such a sweet dog!

7 In General/Generally Speaking
一般而言

This is a very useful tool. Few things in this life are 100%. (Benjamin Franklin said the only things we can be sure of in this life are "death and taxes.") So this is a helpful "hedge" phrase when you are making generalities but are not 100% sure. But just choose one phrase or the other. Do not say, "In generally speaking...."

這是個很好用的片語。人生中很少有百分之百確切的事情（班哲明·富蘭克林說人生可以確定的事只有「死亡和繳稅」）。當你作普遍性推論，但又不是百分之百肯定時，這類「避險」的片語就很好用。但只能選擇其中一個片語來用，不能說 In generally speaking...。

- In general, you hear more Taiwanese in South Taiwan than in the northern parts.

- Generally speaking, the harder you work, the more successful you will be.

8 -ing
動名詞或現在分詞

Many struggle with knowing when to put an "-ing" on a verb. Here are the main times:

很多人對於什麼時候要在動詞後加 -ing 並不清楚，以下是主要的使用時機：

1. As a gerund (a verb acting like a noun) 作動名詞時（作為名詞用的動詞）

- **Swimming** is great exercise.

- **Knowing** when to be quiet is not always easy.

2. With a modal verb (can, should, must, may, etc.) and a be verb
助動詞 (can, should, must, may) 和 be 動詞之後

- The children should be **working** quietly, not **running** around.

- He cannot be **telling** the truth.

- Justin might be **walking** home already.

3. As a future action or future continuous action 表未來的行為或未來進行的行為

- We will be **having** lunch at noon.

- She might be **taking** the writing class this summer.

Here are some Chinglish times to *not* use -ing.

以下是一些中式英文，千萬不要使用 -ing。

1. With "please" 跟 please 連用

- ✘ Please **standing** up.

- ✘ Please **being** quiet!

- ✔ Please stand up.

2. With "to" as an infinitive 加上 to 作為不定詞

- ✘ Do you enjoy **to swimming**?

- ✔ Do you enjoy swimming?

- ✔ Do you enjoy going swimming?

- ✘ We are going **to shopping**.

- ✔ We are going shopping.

- ✔ We will be shopping.

▪ Activity

2.2 Circle the right word from each pair below.

從以下各組字中圈選出正確的字。

1. Do you like (swim/swimming)?

2. I have been (take/taking) (swim/swimming) lessons since I was eight.

3. It is hard to (get/getting) up at six each morning to (go/going) to the pool for practice.

4. But after a while you (get/getting) used to it.

5. I really appreciate my Mom (drive/driving) me to the pool each day.

(Answers are in the Answer Key on page 196.)

9 Nouns Doing the Work of Verbs (Avoid overusing Verb + Noun)

將名詞轉化爲動詞使用（避免過度使用「動詞＋名詞」）

Not only does this let you cut one word, it also makes your writing or speaking sound more natural.

這樣不僅可少用一個字，也可以使你的寫作或口說更爲自然。

AVOID	DO THIS
Do exercise regularly to stay healthy.	Exercise regularly to stay healthy.
Take a rest first and then we will go.	Rest first and then we will go.

10 Old People

老人

Whereas the Chinese is simply *lao ren*（老人）, you normally do *not* want to translate this directly. "Old man" does not sound any better, and you certainly do not want to write: "My grandmother is an old man," unless you *really* want to confuse the reader! It is better to say "older people," "senior citizens," or just "seniors." (Yes, "seniors" can cause confusion with people about to leave high school or college, but the context usually makes it clear.)

中文可以說「老人」，但你可不要直接翻譯成 old man，這實在不怎麼好聽，當然你也不要寫出 My grandmother is an old man. 這種句子，除非你是存心讓讀者搞糊塗。比較好的用法是 older people, senior citizens 或 seniors（當然 seniors 也可能會讓人誤會成是高三或大四的高年級學生，但是上下文通常可以讓人釐清意義）。

- With the advances in medical technology, many older people are living longer nowadays.

- Senior citizens are as a group a big voting bloc in the U.S. and politicians who want to keep their jobs better not make them angry!

- Seniors are living more active lives now than ever before. Former President Bush jumped out of an airplane with a parachute on his 80th birthday—just for fun!

11 Owing to
由於

This is another one of those English phrases that Chinese often use—but native English speakers seldom do. Try replacing it with "due to" or "thanks to." You can sometimes just use "because of" or "since" as well.

這是另一個華人常用、但英美人士卻很少使用的英文片語，可以改用 due to 或 thanks to，有時也可用 because of 或 since。

Rather **Chinglish**:

相當中文式的英文：

- **Owing to** the recent increases in technology, cell phones can do more than ever.
- **Owing to** the rain, we have cancelled the picnic. Sorry.

Change to:

改寫成以下句子：

- Thanks to the recent increases in technology, cell phones can do more than ever.
- Due to the rain, we have cancelled the picnic. Sorry.
- Because of the rain, we have cancelled the picnic. Sorry.
- Since it is raining, we have cancelled the picnic. Sorry.

12 Parts of Speech
詞性

This is not a problem in Chinese, but it can be in English. A friend once told me, "Be careful when you drive in Taiwan! Very danger!" He was kind-hearted to warn me, but of course he meant to say "Very *dangerous*!"

中文裡沒有這種問題，但在英文中就容易出錯。有朋友曾經跟我說 Be careful when you drive in Taiwan! Very danger!，他是出於善意警告我，只是他應該說 Very dangerous!。

Let us review: 我們來複習一下：

danger: (noun)

• This world is full of danger; be careful what you do and where you go.

• If you ever feel in danger, try to get help right away.

dangerous: (adjective—modifies a noun)

• Drinking and driving is very dangerous; do not do it!

• Try to avoid dangerous people and situations.

dangerously: (adverb—modifies a verb)

• He was driving dangerously, so the police arrested him.

• Some people get a thrill out of living dangerously.

(Hint: Adverbs often end in -ly, but not always.)

Activity

2.3 Now you try some: Choose the best word to complete each sentence. In the blank, write in the Part of Speech (verb, noun, adjective, or adverb).

現在換你來試試看：圈選適當的字，並在空格內填入詞性（如動詞、名詞、形容詞或副詞）。

Example: We live in a (safe/safely) neighborhood. _____adjective_____

1. Carry the knife (safe/safely) so you will not get hurt. _____

2. Ah, I love the peace and (quiet/quietly) of the country! _____

3. Shh, speak (quiet/quietly) so you will not wake up Dad. _____

4. Do not (anger/angry/angrily) the neighbor's dog or it may bark for an hour.

   _____

5. Adults should be (gentleness/gentle/gently) around children, so they will feel safe.

   _____

6. "Hold your baby brother (gentleness/gentle/gently)," Mom told Miriam.

   _____

7. Some drivers have so much (anger/angry/angrily) these days; it is frightening!

   _____

8. "We wish you every (happy/happiness/happily) in your married life," Mr. and Mrs. Chin wished the newly-weds. _____

9. "Do not be so nosy," the teacher (anger/angry/angrily) snapped at the curious child.

   _____

10. Do not be (nervousness/nervous/nervously). Your English is getting better step by step! _____

(Answers are in the Answer Key on page 196.)

2.4 Now, you create some sentences with these words:

接下來試著用以下的字來造句：

1. happily _____

2. angrily _____

3. nervous _____

4. dangerously _____

5. sad _____

(Suggested answers are in the Answer Key on page 197.)

13 People and Nationalities
人民與國籍

Chinese is wonderfully simple with this. Just say the name of the place, and tack *ren*（人）onto it, and presto! You have the resident or nationality! But alas, English is not so simple. In fact, the English rule for this is downright crazy, because there is no single rule!

中文在這方面非常單純，只要在國家後面加個「人」字，一下就能寫出該國家的人民或國籍了。但哎～英文可就沒這麼簡單了！事實上，英文的規則可會令人抓狂，因爲根本沒有規則可言。

While the Chinese call themselves *chung guo ren*（中國人）, and you *can* say "Chinese people" in English, it is better to just say "Chinese." Likewise, rather than say "American people," say "Americans;" rather than "Korean people," say "Koreans." Sometimes it sounds better to add "the" before the name, like "Americans like coffee, but <u>the</u> British prefer their tea," especially when you are referring to a nationality as a whole group.

中國人可以自稱爲 chung guo ren，英文可翻成 Chinese people，其實較佳的說法是 Chinese 就好。同樣地，不要說 American people，說 Americans 即可；不要說 Korean people，只說 Koreans 就好了。有時可以在國籍前加 the，例如 Americans like coffee, but the British prefer their tea.，尤其當你指涉的是全體國民時。

The "default setting" for this problem is to add an -s or -ns to the end of the place, but sometimes you add an -ers, or even an -ians. For example, my hometown is Roanoke, Virginia, so people there are called *Roanokers*, but people from my state are called *Virginians*. Residents of Boston, Massachusetts are called *Bostonians*. If you feel confused, join the club; we all are.

解決這個問題的常見方式是在國家後面加 -s 或 -ns，但有時候是要加 -ers 或甚至 -ians。例如我的家鄉是維吉尼亞州的 Roanoke，當地的居民就被稱爲 Roanokers，然而所有維吉尼亞州的人卻被稱爲 Virginians。而住在麻薩諸塞州波士頓的人被稱爲 Bostonians。如果你覺得困惑，你不會寂寞的，因爲連我們都覺得很困惑。

Here is a partial list to get you started:

以下這些例子，可以讓你有個概念：

PLACE		WHAT YOU CALL THE PEOPLE
Australia		Australian(s)
Canada		Canadian(s)
France		French
Germany		German(s)
New Zealand		New Zealander(s)
The Philippines		Filipino(s) But females are called *Filipina(s)*
Russia		Russian(s)
Singapore		Singaporean(s)
Vietnam		Vietnamese

14 Phenomenon
現象

This word is a fine English word, yes, but it is formal and not often used. Chinese speakers use it more than most native English speakers do!

這是個很好的英文字，但它比較正式而且少用，反而華人使用此字比英美人士頻繁。例如以下的中式英文：

- My girlfriend will not return my phone calls. Have you ever experienced this phenomenon before? (**Chinglish**)

Instead, use words like *happen, occur, experience* or *tendency*.

其實應該使用如 happen, occur, experience 或 tendency 等字較適切。

- My girlfriend will not return my phone calls. Has this ever happened to you before?

- Florida seldom gets snow, but it has happened before. (*or* it has occurred before.)

- I just had a strange experience: I saw a mailman try to bite a dog!

Activity

2.5 You do it:

改寫以下的句子：

1. I slept ten hours but when I woke up I still felt tired. <u>Have you ever experienced this phenomenon?</u>

_____

2. Some people say jet lag is annoying. <u>Have you ever experienced this phenomenon before?</u>

_____

3. Culture shock is a common phenomenon.

_____

(Suggested answers are in the Answer Key on page 197.)

15 Place Names With or Without *The*
加 the 與不加 the 的地名

This too is not an issue in Chinese, but it is in English. Here are a few simple rules:

中文裡同樣沒有這個問題，但在英文中就讓人很頭痛，以下有幾個簡單的規則：

1. Continents: Do <u>not</u> use *the*. 世界五大洲不加 the

✗ I am going to **the** Europe next spring.

✔ I am going to Europe next spring.

2. Regions: This gets tricky. 地區就比較複雜了

A) Use *the* for these regions:

以下這些地區要加 the：

- Violence is so common in the Middle East.

- Many westerners are fascinated by the Far East: China, Japan, and Korea.

- The Caribbean is a melting pot of many cultures, languages, and ethnicities: English, French, Dutch, African, Hispanic, and Native American.

- The Midwest—covering the area from Ohio to Iowa and Minnesota—is home to both heavy industry and agriculture.

B) But do <u>not</u> use *the* with these regions:

但以下這些地區不需要加 the：

- Vietnam is in Southeast Asia.

- Central America is home to seven small countries.

- New England is the area in the U.S. between Connecticut and Maine.

C) Do <u>not</u> use *the* when you say a compass direction, as an adjective, before a region.

地名前有表示方向的形容詞時不要加 the。

- Southern Taiwan is warm almost all year round.

- Have you ever been to western Canada? It is gorgeous!

- Eastern China is home to almost one billion people.

- Western Europe is one of the world's wealthiest areas.

D) Deserts are a kind of region. Use *the* when naming either a specific desert or referring to a desert in general.

沙漠也是種地區，不論指特定的沙漠或是一般的沙漠都要加 the。

- The Sahara is the world's largest desert.

- The Gobi Desert straddles the border between China and Mongolia.

- The desert has strange weather: it can be blazing hot during the day but freezing cold at night!

3. Counties, States, Provinces and Countries: Generally do <u>not</u> use *the*.

郡縣、州、省和國家前通常不加 the

✗ I would love to go to **the** Germany someday!

✔ I would love to go to Germany someday!

✗ **The** Nantou County is in the center of **the** Taiwan.

✔ Nantou County is in the center of Taiwan.

✗ **The** Sichuan Province in **the** China has more people than in all of **the** France!

✔ Sichuan Province in China has more people than in all of France!

Exception: Do you know what the world's smallest country is? It is both a country and a city. It is the Vatican (and it requires a *the*).

例外：你知道全世界最小的國家是哪一國嗎？它既是一個國家，也是一個城市，那就是梵諦岡（前面要加 the）。

- The Pope, leader of the world's one billion Catholics, lives in the Vatican.

4. Countries with "kingdom," "republic," "states," or plural names. These <u>do</u> have *the*. 國家名稱中具有 kingdom, republic, states 等字，或是複數名詞，就要加 the

- Mao Zedong formed the People's Republic of China in 1949.

- South Korea's official name is the Republic of Korea.

- The Philippines has some 7,000 islands! (But note the singular verb, *has*.)

5. Cities and Towns generally do <u>not</u> use *the*. 城市和鄉鎮通常不加 the

✗ Her parents live in **the** Vancouver.

✔ Her parents live in Vancouver.

Exception:

- The Vatican, though tiny, is both a city and a country!

6. Islands 島嶼

A) Island chains with plural names usually have *the*.

具有複數型的群島通常要加 the。

- The British Isles are the birthplace of the English language.

- The Spratly Islands are claimed by six countries: Mainland China, Taiwan, the Philippines, Vietnam, Malaysia, and Brunei! What a recipe for conflict!

B) A single island usually does <u>not</u> have *the*.

單獨的島嶼通常不加 the。

- Orchid Island is known for its aboriginal culture.

- Green Island has one of the world's only hot springs *inside* the ocean!

- I have always dreamed of visiting Bermuda!

7. **Mountains** 山脈

A) Mountain ranges with plural names usually have *the*.

具有複數型的山脈通常要加 the。

- The Alps in Europe are known for their natural beauty—and high prices!

- The Blue Ridge Mountains of Virginia are beautiful, especially when the colors change.

- Our wealthy friends often go skiing in the Colorado Rockies each winter.

B) A single mountain usually does <u>not</u> use *the*.

單獨的山岳通常不加 the。

- Mount Fuji is the most famous mountain in Japan.

- The new tunnel through Snow Mountain has cut the travel time between Taipei and Ilan.

- Taipei's Yangming Mountain is known for its beautiful spring flowers and hot springs.

8. **Oceans, Seas, Rivers, Straits, Swamps and Canals. These generally <u>do</u> use *the*.** 海洋、河流、海峽、沼澤和運河等通常要加 the

- The Pacific Ocean
- The Taiwan Strait
- The Sea of Japan
- The Everglades
- The Yellow River
- The Mediterranean Sea
- The East China Sea
- The Dismal Swamp
- The English Channel
- The Gulf of Mexico
- The Mississippi River
- The Panama Canal

9. **Lakes. These usually do <u>not</u> use *the*.** 湖泊通常不加 the

- Sun Moon Lake is a popular tourist destination in Central Taiwan.

- Smith Mountain Lake is a pretty spot in Virginia.

Exception: The Great Lakes on the U.S./Canada border need *the* when considered as <u>one unit</u>.

- The five Great Lakes can be remembered with the acronym HOMES: Huron, Ontario, Michigan, Erie, and Superior.

10. Streets, Roads, and Squares. Generally do <u>not</u> use *the*.

街、路和廣場名通常不加 the

- Tienanmen Square in Beijing literally translates as "Gate of Heavenly Peace."

- Hong Kong's Nathan Street is a popular shopping district.

- Park Avenue is a coveted address in New York City.

11. Famous museums, buildings and monuments. These usually <u>do</u> have *the*. 有名的博物館、建築物和紀念碑通常要加 the

- The National Palace Museum in Taipei is the world's most famous site for ancient Chinese art.

- Everyone knows that the U.S. president lives in the White House.

- Can we meet at the Hilton across from the Taipei Train Station?

- The Berlin Wall and the Iron Curtain were ugly reminders that communism does not give people freedom.

- The Statue of Liberty, a gift from France, has long greeted immigrants to the United States.

Places with *of* in the name usually have *the* also.

有加 of 的地名通常也要加 the。

- The Great Wall of China
- The Museum of Natural History
- The University of Virginia
- The University of California at Los Angeles

Note: Rule 11 applies to <u>famous</u> places. So you can say "Meet me at the Hilton," but not "Meet me at the McDonald's." As is so often the case with English, though, there is an exception to this rule also. Use *the* when you refer to a specific person or place, to distinguish it from another or to avoid confusion.

Example. You may say "Please meet me at McDonald's" if there is <u>only one</u> McDonald's in town. But what if there are several? That's when you use *the* plus a specific direction.

注意：規則 11 適用於有名的地方，例如你可以說 Meet me at the Hilton.，但不可以說 Meet me at the McDonald's.。不過英文經常都有例外，所以這條規則也是一樣，當你要指涉一個特定的人或地方以便區分其他人或地方、或是要避免混淆時就要加 the。

例如城裡如果只有一家麥當勞時，你可以說 Please meet me at McDonald's.，但如果是有數家麥當勞的話，那你就要加 the 和特定的說明。

- Please meet me at the McDonald's across from the Science Park.
- I'll meet you at the 7-11 at the corner of School House Road and Bwo Ai Lane.
- My kids will be waiting for you at the RT-Mart near Kuang-fu Road.

12. Named storm 命名的颱風

Even though these are storms, not places, you should know about them. They do <u>not</u> use *the*.

雖然這些是颱風名，而不是地名，你也應該知道它們不加 the。

- Typhoon Wanda killed thousands in China during the 1950s.
- New Orleans has never fully recovered from Hurricane Katrina in 2005.

13. Software 電腦軟體名

This is not a place name either, but this might help you. For software (Microsoft, Excel, etc.), do <u>not</u> use *the* unless you use it as an adjective and use a word like "spreadsheet" or "software" after it.

這也不是地名，但你也需要知道軟體名（如微軟、Excel 等）前不加 the，除非你把它當作形容詞，後面還跟著像 spreadsheet 或 software 等字時。

✘ Download the data to **the** Excel.

✔ Download the data to Excel.

✔ Download the data to the Excel spreadsheet.

✔ Do you have the new Word software?

To **The** *or Not to* **The,** *That is the Question!*   加 the，或不加 the，這真是大哉問！

■ Activity

2.6 Now that you have reviewed when to use *the* with place names, add in *the* where needed below. If no *the* is needed, leave the space blank.

你已學過何時該在地名前加 the，請在以下句中需要的地方加上 the，如果不需要加 the，就不用填寫該空格。

1. Mary is a sweet woman from _____ Philippines.

2. Most Filipinos live on _____ Luzon, the main island where the capital, Manila, is located.

3. Taiwan's official name is _____ Republic of China, or R.O.C. for short.

4. _____ Taipei is Taiwan's capital.

5. _____ Tsing Hua University, Taiwan's top engineering school, is in Hsinchu.

6. _____ Science Park, home to many high-tech industries, is in Hsinchu also.

7. _____ SuAo Highway between Taipei and Ilan has beautiful views of _____ Pacific Ocean, but it can be dangerous!

8. _____ Ali Mountain is well-known for its sunrise views.

9. Taiwan can get bad typhoons but fortunately _____ high Central Mountains normally block the storms and keep _____ western part of Taiwan relatively calm.

10. Taiwan and _____ Mainland China both touch _____ South China Sea.

11. Most people agree that _____ East Taiwan has the prettiest scenery.

12. After a trip around Taiwan, it is fun to grab a cup of tea at _____ Taipei Hilton and relax before going home.

(Answers are in the Answer Key on page 197.)

16 Possessives
所有格

Cut unnecessary "of" phrases. Use possessives instead to reduce your word count.

刪除片語中不必要的 of，使用所有格來精簡字數。

WORDY	The **drawback of the design** is that it requires more memory.
BETTER	The design's drawback is that it requires more memory.

WORDY	The **tail of the dog** was wagging.
BETTER	The dog's tail was wagging.

17 Relax Your Mind
放鬆你的心情

• Go out with your friends and relax your mind. (**Chinglish**)

Instead, say "take it easy" or "relax for a while."

應該改成 take it easy 或 relax for a while。

• Do not be so hard on yourself; just take it easy!

• Hey, you have been studying for five hours and it is already midnight; take it easy and go on to bed. You will feel fresher in the morning.

■ Activity

2.7 You do it:

改寫以下的句子：

1. Go relax your mind and go for a walk.

_____

2. I know you are upset that your girlfriend dumped you, but relax your mind. You'll find somebody else.

_____

3. Studying for test is hard, but it is important to relax your mind some.

_____

(Suggested answers are in the Answer Key on page 198.)

18 Smiling Face
微笑的臉

- When people see your smiling face, they will know you are easy-going.
  (**Chinglish**)

Instead, say "smile."   應該說 smile 就可以了。

- When people see your smile, they will know you are easy-going.
- Keep your smile and your day will go better.

Activity

2.8 You do it:

改寫以下的句子：

1. Your smiling face will draw people to you.

_____

2. Everyone liked Annie because of her smiling face.

_____

3. Wear a smiling face while you are giving a speech, and your audience will probably like you more.

_____

(Suggested answers are in the Answer Key on page 198.)

19 Studies
研究

This noun can replace "research."

此名詞可取代 research。

- Many **researches** on this topic have been helpful. (**Chinglish**)
- Many studies on this topic have been helpful. (**Correct**)

20 Subject/Verb Agreement
主詞與動詞的一致性

This is not an issue in Chinese grammar, but it is *a big deal* in English; it even troubles native English speakers! The subject of your sentence must always match the verb form! Here is a tip: usually, <u>an -s at the end of a noun makes it plural</u> (factories), while <u>an -s at the end of a verb makes it singular</u> (produces). This is not always true, but this occurs in grammar more often than not. (Irregular verbs like "to be" do not follow the -s rule, but they are the exception.) Some examples:

這在中文不會造成困擾，但在英文裡問題就大了，甚至連英語母語人士都感到頭大。句子的主詞必須與動詞的單複數一致，這裡有個祕訣：通常名詞後有 -s 就是複數（如 dogs），而動詞後有 -s 則是單數（如 walks）。這個祕訣並不是絕對的，但文法中大部分的情況是如此（不規則動詞就不遵循 -s 的規則，例如 to be，但它們是例外）。如以下例句：

- The factory produces computers. (singular)
- The factories produce computers. (plural)

You can never write or say: "The factories produces computers." Get it?

你絕不能寫或說成 The factories produces computers.，懂了嗎？

Here are some examples; a few include irregular verbs, just for the challenge.

以下還有一些例句，少數是用不規則動詞，就當作是種挑戰吧。

✘ I **is** learning English.

✔ I am learning English. (singular)

✘ The name "Formosa" **mean** "Beautiful Island" in Portuguese.

✔ The name "Formosa" means "Beautiful Island" in Portuguese. (singular)

✘ Christmas trees **is** a big part of the Christmas celebration in America.

✔ Christmas trees are a big part of the Christmas celebration in America. (plural)

▪ Activity

2.9 Now, look these over and put a (✔) by sentences with correct subject/verb agreement, and an (✖) by those that are wrong.

閱讀以下的句子，在主詞和動詞一致性正確的句子前打 ✔，錯誤的則打 ✖。

1. _____ The Chinese is known for their good work ethic.

2. _____ Education are valued in most Chinese families.

3. _____ Dragon Boat Festival, Mid-Autumn Festival, and Chinese New Year are the biggest holidays in the Chinese calendar.

4. _____ Watching fish swim in an aquarium have been proven to reduce blood pressure.

5. _____ Seafood are a big part of the Japanese diet.

6. _____ Your professors and teachers want you to do well in school.

7. _____ The United States are a big country.

8. _____ Getting enough money to buy a house is not easy; start saving early!

9. _____ The ducks is swimming gracefully.

10. _____ "Children is a blessing from the Lord," the Bible say.

(Answers are in the Answer Key on page 198.)

21 Verb + -ing
動詞 + -ing

Do not overuse "To + Infinitive"; instead, add "-ing" to the verb. The To + Infinitive Construction is helpful, but many times you can just cut the "to" and add an "ing" to the end of the verb; this sounds more natural. English teachers call this a "gerund," and this is a neat trick to make a verb do the work of a noun.

不要過度使用「to + 不定詞」，在動詞加上 ing 即可。「To + 不定詞」的結構是很有用，但在很多情況下你只要把 to 去掉，再於動詞後加上 ing，這樣才比較自然。英文老師稱這種結構為動名詞，是把動詞變成名詞的好技巧。例如：

AVOID	DO THIS
To build friendships is not easy.	Building friendships is not easy.
To swim is healthy.	Swimming is healthy.
To raise children is hard work.	Raising children is hard work.
To watch birds is relaxing.	Watching birds is relaxing. *Or* Bird watching is relaxing.
To smile requires fewer muscles than **to frown**.	Smiling requires fewer muscles than frowning.

Activity

2.10 Now, you try some:

現在你來練習看看：

AVOID	DO THIS
1. To learn English takes time.	
2. To read is good for your mind.	
3. To watch TV can be a waste of time.	
4. To have a pet can keep older people healthy.	

(Answers are in the Answer Key on page 199.)

Part C

Twelve Steps to
Clearer Writing
精進寫作的12步驟

Twelve Steps to Clearer Writing
精進寫作的 12 步驟

And now, the actual twelve steps!

現在，正式開始實戰的寫作 12 步驟！

1 Start Strong
有力的開始

Think about what you want to say 你要寫什麼？

This may sound funny, but the first part of writing does not start with writing at all! It involves *thinking*. Yes, *thinking about what you want to write*. It is also called *brainstorming*. The fact that you are reading this book tells me you want to write; however, picking a topic and getting started can be hard. Sometimes your teacher assigns you a topic, so you have no choice: such as when you have to write a report on, say, Mongolia. But even for people who *want* to write, finding your topic can be hard. If you have to write a book report, try to find a book that interests you. If you are to write a report on a city, pick a place you would love to visit. If you are writing a journal or some fiction, then you have almost complete freedom on what you write. But before writing, <u>first think about what you want to say</u>.

這聽起來蠻有趣的，寫作的第一步竟然不是開始動筆寫，而是要思考。是的，思考你要寫什麼，或稱為腦力激盪。你閱讀這本書的原因當然就是你想要寫作，然而要挑個題目開始動筆寫可沒那麼容易。有時你的老師會指定作文題目，例如要你針對蒙古寫份報告，你根本沒有選擇的餘地。但即使是自己有心寫作，找題目也是件難事。如果你要寫份讀書報告，就要找本你有興趣的書；如果你要寫份城市的報告，你也要選個想要參訪的城市；如果你要寫日誌或小說，那你的寫作型式就十分隨性。總之，在寫作之前，首先要思考你想表達的東西。

An outline 大綱

Once you have in mind the *general* idea of what you want to say, "Why I love Tigers" or "My Dream is to

一旦你心中有了想法，比如說「我為何喜歡老虎」或「我的夢想是將來到土耳其旅遊」，那你就可以開始

Visit Turkey Someday," *then* you can start writing things down. Many people, before they start writing text, first like to create an <u>outline</u> or <u>chart</u> of what they want to say. For example, *this book began as just one sheet of paper*, a simple outline of the 12 steps! You can see one student's outline, about obesity, on page 53. Some people like a Venn Diagram or Web. Below are some examples.

下筆。許多人在寫作前會先擬定大綱或表格,例如這本書的雛型就只是一張紙,上面簡單列出 12 個步驟的綱要。你也可以參考第 53 頁由一名同學所寫的「肥胖」一文的大綱。也有些人喜歡先畫個范恩圖或網狀圖。以下就是這兩種圖表的例子:

VENN DIAGRAM
范恩圖

Comparing and contrasting Taipei and Kaohsiung
台北和高雄的比較和對照

TAIPEI
North Taiwan
hear more Mandarin
larger population
more foreigners
surrounded by mountains
colder winters

major cities
much shopping
business centers
lots to do

KAOHSIUNG
South Taiwan
hear more Taiwanese
fewer people than
Taipei
fewer foreigners
fewer mountains
warmer winters

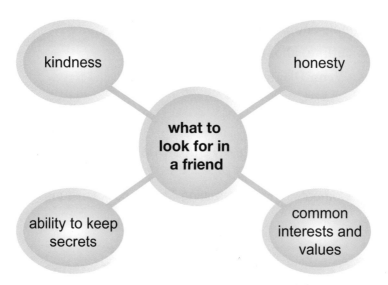

WEB
網狀圖

Traits to look for in a friend
朋友的特質

Once you have brainstormed and made an outline or chart of main ideas, you can begin with your text.

等你腦力激盪完並就主旨擬出大綱或圖表後，就可以開始撰寫本文。

A catchy title 醒目的題目

The beginning of your paper is crucial. Your teachers at school basically *must* read what you write, but out in the "real world" (whatever that is), if someone starts to read your article but finds it dull or unclear, he will skip it and go on elsewhere. The average reader will give your work just a few seconds and decide whether to keep reading or skip it. So catch your reader's attention.

文章的開頭很重要，學校的老師基本上是一定得讀你的作品，但是在「現實世界」裡（無論是何種情況），如果有人一讀你的文章就覺得無趣或不知所云，他可是會懶得再看下去而改做其他事情。一般人只花幾十秒閱讀你的作品，就可以決定要繼續閱讀或將它丟到一旁。所以切記，要引起讀者的興趣。

For example, for many standardized tests such as the TOEFL or GRE, the essay readers are allotted just <u>three minutes per essay</u>, and they read 100-200 essays per

例如許多標準化測驗像托福或 GRE，閱卷者批改每篇文章只花三分鐘，而每次要批閱 100 到 200 份作文！在這種閱卷情況下，你必須讓你的作

session! Against odds like this, you *must* make a good first impression and stand out!

文脫穎而出，讓人留下良好的第一印象。

First, get a catchy title.

首先，找個引人注意的題目。

You should first check with your teacher about what he or she wants in a title, but in general, *do* have a title, and make it clever.

你應該先詢問老師對題目有何意見，一般來說一定要有個題目，而且要讓它看起來很出色。

How do these titles grab you? Do they make you want to keep reading?

以下這些題目會吸引你嗎？它們會讓你想繼續讀下去嗎？

- English Essay
- Essay for Mrs. Brown
- Research Paper for History Class

What is wrong? They are boring.

這些題目有什麼問題呢？它們都太無趣了。

Sometimes your title can be a play on words. For instance, Habitat for Humanity is a Christian organization dedicated to using volunteer labor to build homes for the poor (former U.S. President Jimmy Carter is a supporter). To introduce their work to young readers, the organization produced a children's book called *Raising the Roof*. This is a play on words: "raising the roof" literally means to build a building, but it also means to have a good time, a big party. So, the title was great, because the story is about people who built a house for free, and had fun doing it.

有時你的題目可以玩些文字遊戲，例如「人道家園」是個基督教組織，由義工為窮人建造房屋（美國前總統卡特是支持者），為了向小讀者介紹他們的工作而發行的兒童刊物稱為《Raising the Roof》，這個書名就是在玩文字遊戲：就字面上而言，它是指蓋房子，但也可以指一段歡樂時光或一個大型派對。所以這個書名就很棒，因為裡面的故事都是有關人們免費幫窮人建造房屋，同時在過程中也享有美好的時光。

Or maybe you are writing about a musician. A clever title might be "Playing Around," because "playing around" means "to have fun," but it is also a pun because the musician plays instruments. Think and try to be creative.

或者你想寫篇有關音樂家的文章，題目訂為「Playing Around」就蠻不錯，因為它意謂著歡樂，而同時也是個雙關語，可以指音樂家演奏樂器。總之要思考並試著有創意。

A hook 切入點

<u>So once you have your title, you next want a "hook."</u> This is the opening of your paper. It has to hook, or grab, the reader's attention.

有了題目之後，接著就需要一個「切入點」來作為文章的開頭，以吸引讀者的注意。

1. Questions 問題

Questions make great hooks. Some examples are:

問題就是個很好的切入點。例如：

- What do you look for in a friend?

- What is your favorite city?

- Why do you think divorce is so common?

2. Quotation 引言

Another way to create a hook is to start with a quotation.

另一個的方式是以引言作為切入點。

For instance, you could start a paper about greed or materialism with this gem by G.K. Chesterton: *There are two ways to get enough. One is to accumulate more and more. The other is to need less.* If you were writing about the need to plan your life carefully, you may want to start with: *Life is like a coin; you can spend it any way you wish, but you can only spend it once,* by Charles Swindoll.

例如你在撰寫有關貪婪或物質主義的文章時，就可以引用 G.K. Chesterton 的名言來破題：「獲得滿足有兩種方法，一是不斷累積，二是減少需求。」若你是在撰寫有關謹慎規畫生命的議題，開宗明義就可以引用 Charles Swindoll 的話：「生命如同錢幣，可以如你所願花費，但你只能花費一次。」

I am a big fan of quotations. For years I have written down lines I find particularly moving, and I urge you to do the same. So, when you read a great quotation or hear something especially powerful in a speech, go ahead and write it down! Make a Quotations file in your PC. Many great Quotations websites are online, searchable by topic or author.

- www.quotationspage.com
- www.quoteland.com

我很喜歡引言，過去幾年來我抄錄了許多感人的引言，你也可以試試看。當你讀到一些佳句或在演講中聽到令人震撼的句子時，就趕快記下來。你可在電腦中製作一個引言檔案。網路上也有許多不錯的引言網站，可以用主題或作者來檢索。

Activity

3.1 Think for a moment about what kinds of essays you could write if you started with these quotations:

思考一下，用下面這些引言開頭的文章，應該搭配什麼題目：

1. *Don't worry about the world coming to an end today.*
   It's already tomorrow in Australia. —Charles Schultz

   Topic: _____

2. *The strength of a nation derives from the integrity of the home.* —Confucius

   Topic: _____

3. *A nation which does not remember what it was yesterday, does not know what it is today, nor what it is trying to do. We are trying to do a futile thing if we do not know where we came from or what we have been about.* —Woodrow Wilson

   Topic: _____

4. *Work as if you were to live 100 years, Pray as if you were to die tomorrow.*
   —Benjamin Franklin, in *Poor Richard's Almanack*, 1757.

   Topic: _____

5. *Diamonds are nothing more than chunks of coal that stuck to their jobs.*
   —Malcolm Forbes

   Topic: _____

6. *Security is mostly a superstition. It does not exist in nature, nor do the children of men as a whole experience it. Avoiding danger is no safer in the long run than outright exposure. Life is either a daring adventure, or nothing.* —Helen Keller

   Topic: _____

(Suggested answers are in the Answer Key on page 199.)

3. Surprising or mysterious things 令人感到驚奇或懸疑的事

A third way to create a hook is to say something surprising or mysterious.

創造切入點的第三個方式是寫出令人感到驚奇或懸疑的東西。

I love how James Mitchner opened his classic, *Chesapeake*:

我很喜歡 James Mitchner 在他的經典作品《Chesapeake》的開場：

- They had been watching him for a long time.

Does that make you want to keep reading? It did me, and it kept me going through the thousand-some pages!

這種寫法是不是會誘使你繼續往下讀？我就是受到吸引才連看了上千頁。

How about this opener from parenting commentator John Rosemond?

以下是教養子女的評論家 John Rosemond 所寫的開場白：

- I believe in low self-esteem.

Does that make you want to keep reading? Whether you agree or disagree with Rosemond's point, his claim is provocative and sparks curiosity.

這句話是否也會促使你讀下去？不論你同不同意 Rosemond 的觀點，他挑釁的說法已經引發人們的好奇心。

4. Statistics 數據

A fourth way to launch a paper is to cite a statistic.

第四種開展文章的方式是引用數據。

- The world's biggest Muslim country is not Saudi Arabia, Egypt, or Pakistan: it is Indonesia.
- Mainland China has about as many people learning English as there are total inhabitants in the United States of America!

5. Joke or short story 笑話或小故事

You can also begin with a joke or short story.

你也可以用笑話或小故事作為開頭。

Cecil Osborne, in his book *The Art of Getting Along with People*, starts with both a quotation *and* a funny story.

Cecil Osborne 所著的《The Art of Getting Along with People》一書就是以引言和一個有趣的小故事來揭開序幕。

Patience is the ability to put up with people you'd like to put down.

—Ulrike Ruffer

A woman once asked a ninety-one-year-old friend why he had chosen to retire to a small Indiana town of five thousand instead of to Indianapolis [the state capital], where there would be more to do and see.

He replied, "If I were to drop dead one day in downtown Indianapolis, everybody would just step over me and go about their business. If I were to drop dead here, everyone would step over me and go about their business—but they'd say, "There's old Tom Clark."

Osborne then gets serious and makes his point, by continuing:

Osborne 接下來就以比較正經的口吻闡述他的重點：

- This man's facetious but apt comment points up an important facet of human nature: *We all want to be noticed.* No one wants to be ignored or forgotten or to die unrecognized.[1]

Do you see how Osborne made his point? What if he had just begun his book with "We all want to be noticed"? Would that have been a stronger, or weaker, introduction?

你注意到 Osborne 是如何帶出他的重點了嗎？如果他是以 We all want to be noticed. 作為書的開頭，這樣的寫法是會強化還是削弱開頭的力道？

As with quotations, keep your eyes open for good stories you read or hear. Take mental notes, or even better, write the story down and use it yourself! Thanks

就像抄錄引言一樣，對於好的故事也要保持耳目暢通，你可以記在心裡，最好還可以把故事寫下來，以備不時之需。由於網路發達，很容

---

1 Osborne, Cecil G. *The Art of Getting Along with People.* Grand Rapids, MI: Zondervan, 1980. p. 9.

to the miracle of the Internet, many of these stories are now available. A search for "Sermon Illustrations," for example, can give you countless stories and anecdotes, on topics from Anger to Zeal.

易搜尋到許多故事，例如你可以查一下 Sermon Illustrations，就可看到無數的故事和趣聞，主題從憤怒到熱忱都找得到。

Activity

3.2 Now you do it: Take these boring titles and juice them up.

現在換你練習看看：把無趣的題目改得生動活潑一些。

Example: Pollution (*boring*) → Slow-Motion Suicide (*better*)

1. The Invention of the Telephone → _____

2. Henry Ford → _____

3. Pearl Harbor → _____

4. My Favorite Hobby → _____

(Suggested answers are in the Answer Key on page 200.)

Introductory paragraph and thesis statement 首段與主旨句

"Starting Strong" in your writing has several steps. Let us review: First, brainstorm to get the general idea of what you want to say. Second, make an outline or web to identify your main points. Third, develop a catchy title. (If you are having trouble here, do not panic. You can always change your title. For that matter, you can always change anything you write! Also, some people write the text first, then choose the title last, after they see what they have created. It is up to you.) Fourth, pick a "hook" to grab the reader. Once you have thought of the hook, craft the first paragraph. This rule is flexible, but a paragraph is generally five to eight sentences. This is the introduction to your paper, where you set the stage or introduce your topic. Somewhere, usually in this first paragraph, you will need a thesis statement. A thesis statement is simply the main idea you are trying to prove in your writing.

Below is Kathleen T. McWhorter's fine explanation of a thesis statement, in her own words.

What is a thesis statement? 何謂主旨句？

A thesis statement is the main point of an essay; it identifies and explains what the essay will be about and often gives clues about how the essay will develop. Usually it is expressed in a single sentence. Think of a thesis statement as a promise to your reader. The rest of your essay delivers on your promise.

寫作的「有力的開始」包括幾個步驟，我們先回顧一下：首先腦力激盪出你想表達的意見。第二步是擬出寫作大綱或網狀圖以確認重點。第三步是想出一個搶眼的題目（如果一時缺乏靈感，無需驚慌，你隨時都可以更改題目。其實，文章的每一部分都可以改。有些人是先寫本文，待審視完全文，最後再想題目。這可由你自行決定。）第四就是要找個切入點來吸引讀者，等你想好了就可開始撰寫第一段。一段通常包含五到八個句子，但這個規則很有彈性。第一段旨在介紹你的文章，搭建舞台來引導出你的主旨。通常在文章的首段要寫出主旨句，也就是你寫作的主要重點。

以下是 Kathleen T. McWhorter 對於主旨句的解釋：

主旨句是一篇文章的主要重點，它指出並解釋這篇文章的內容，並可提供文章發展的線索。它通常可用一個句子來表達，把主旨句視為你對讀者的承諾，文中的其他部分就是要來兌現這個承諾。

Here is a sample thesis statement.

以下是主旨句的例子：

- Playing team sports, especially football and baseball, develops skills and qualities that can make you successful in life because these sports demand communication, teamwork, and responsibility.

In this thesis, the writer promises to show how team sports, especially football and baseball, equip players with important skills and qualities. The reader, then, expects to discover what skills and qualities football and baseball players learn and how these contribute to success in life.

在此主旨句中，作者承諾要告訴讀者團體運動——特別是足球和棒球，如何培養球員重要的技能和特質。讀者會預期讀到球員究竟能學到何種技能和特質，以及這些技能和特質如何導致成功的人生。

Developing your thesis statement 撰寫你的主旨句

Once in a while, for a topic that you are interested in and familiar with, a thesis may come to you immediately. Most of the time, however, you will not be able simply to sit down and write a thesis statement. Usually, a thesis statement needs to evolve or develop as you explore your topic during prewriting. In addition to prewriting, for some topics you will need to do research to develop a thesis. You may need to consult library sources, interview an expert, search the World Wide Web, or check statistics in an almanac, for example. Your thesis may change, too, as you work through the process of organizing supporting evidence, drafting, and revising.[2]

對於你有興趣和熟悉的題目，你可能很快就能寫出主旨句。然而在大多數的情況下，你是無法一坐下來就馬上想出一句主旨句的。通常主旨句會在你寫作前構思時，慢慢發展成形。除了寫作前的構思，有些題目需要先作些研究才能發展出主旨句。例如你可能需要到圖書館查詢資料、訪談專家、瀏覽網路、或檢索年鑑上的統計數據等。在你組織論證、撰寫草稿及修訂文章時，你的主旨句也可能因此跟著改變。

As McWhorter put it, do your research and <u>do not be afraid to change your thesis as you find new information and rethink things</u>. For example, a high

如 McWhorter 所言，儘量去研究你的主題，找到新資料或重新思考後，就大膽修訂你的主旨。例如我認識的一名高中女生，她最近要寫一篇有關

---

2 McWhorter, Kathleen T. *Successful College Writing*. Boston, MA: Bedford/St. Martin's, 2000. p. 97

school girl I know was recently writing a report about the United Nations (UN). Her original thesis was about what a *wonderful* organization the UN is and why it needs more money to support it. As she did more research, though, she uncovered many unpleasant facts about the organization. The girl later changed her thesis to why the UN does *not* deserve more money. (And evidently, she wrote clearly and powerfully, because she won the award.)

聯合國的報告。她原本的主旨是主張聯合國是個偉大的組織，需要更多的資金來支持它。但當她深入研究後，發現許多聯合國的不良事蹟，所以她改變原來的主旨，主張聯合國不配獲得更多的資助。（顯然她寫得清楚有力，因爲她的作品得獎了。）

As for the location of your thesis statement, it should be near the top of your paper, probably somewhere in the first paragraph. English teachers argue about this: some say it should be the first sentence in the opening paragraph; others say it should be the second sentence, or even the last sentence, in the first paragraph. Some say it is okay to have it somewhere in the second paragraph. The exact location is not as important as having a thesis statement that is understandable and somewhere near the top of the paper. Main point? Make it crystal clear to your reader where you are taking him or her. Would you like to get into a car and head off to some unknown destination? Probably not. Likewise, your reader wants to know your destination, before getting in with you.

主旨句應該出現在靠近文章開頭的地方，可能是在第一段的某處。很多英文老師對於這點有不同意見：有些人說應該是在首段的第一句，也有人認爲在第二句較佳，甚至也有人主張放在最後一句，另外還有人表示放在第二段也可以。其實主旨句的位置在哪裡不是那麼重要，重要的是只要接近文章開頭，而且清楚易懂。重點在於能夠讓讀者清楚了解文章的走向。就像你不會上車後就開往不知名的目的地吧？同樣地，讀者也希望在和你一起出發前，就知道文章的方向和目的。

Do you know what the world's most widely-read magazine is? *Reader's Digest*. Do you know a big reason for its success? It is clear and readable. Here is a recent gem: pay careful attention to the title, hook, and thesis statement. Do they make you want to keep reading?

你知道全世界最多人閱讀的雜誌是什麼嗎？就是《讀者文摘》。那你知道它廣受歡迎的理由是什麼？因爲它清楚易讀。以下摘錄一篇最近的佳作：注意它的題目、切入點和主旨句，它們會吸引你繼續讀下去嗎？

GAMBLING WITH THEIR LIVES
Young women and a deadly habit. Can they finally quit?
By Patricia Curtis

A dozen twentysomethings gathered at a Manhattan bar. Two were med students, another a PhD candidate at an Ivy League university, and the rest young professionals making their way in the big city. They were the image of health and fitness, except for one thing—10 of the 12 were smokers.

Young people are lighting up in large numbers, especially those 18 to 24. One in five women in this age group nationwide is a smoker, a figure that has held fairly steady for the past few years. Some blame the billions that cigarette companies spend on marketing each year (US$13 billion in '05), including promotions geared toward young adults. Girls are especially influenced by the glamorous images of smokers in movies and shows (...), and many of them have heard that smoking can keep them thin.[3]

1. Look at the title. Does it grab you?

Note how Curtis, the author, has *two* titles—good technique! Notice also that the title does *not mention smoking*. Why? Perhaps Curtis thought that would give it away as "just another anti-smoking article" and readers would skip it. The mystery *is* a draw. "Gambling with their lives." "Deadly habit." Note also the question: "Can they finally quit?"

2. What is the hook?

"A dozen twentysomethings gathered at a Manhattan bar." Does that make you curious to read more? Who

1. 這題目會吸引你嗎？

作者 Curtis 使用兩個標題，這是個好技巧。而且注意題目本身並沒有講到吸菸，為什麼呢？也許 Curtis 認為這樣會透露出「這又是一篇反菸文章」的老調，讀者就會跳過去不想看了。關鍵是要吸引讀者注意。Gambling with their lives. 和 deadly habit 等字眼以及 Can they finally quit? 的問題都能讓人提起興趣。

2. 切入點在哪裡？

就是這句 A dozen twentysomethings gathered at a Manhattan bar.，這會引起你的好奇，進而想了解更多

3 Curtis, Patricia. *Reader's Digest*, "Gambling with their Lives," Jan. 2008. pp. 140-141.

are they? Why are they at a bar in New York City? Are they pretty? The hook sets the scene, but it does *not* give away the topic. Curtis waits until the end of the first paragraph to raise the curtain: this article is about *smoking.*

3. What is the thesis statement?

"Young people are lighting up in large numbers, especially those 18 to 24." So this article is not just about the 10 young women in New York; *it is about smoking among young adults in general.* Curtis just used the young women in the bar to hook us into the story, to put a "human face" on the problem.

Now, just for fun, imagine rewriting the article this way.

內情嗎？這些人是誰？他們為什麼在紐約市的酒吧裡？她們漂亮嗎？這個切入角度把場景點出來，但還沒講出題目是什麼。Curtis 要等到第一段結束時才揭開序幕：這是篇有關吸菸的文章。

3. 主旨句在哪裡？

就是這句 Young people are lighting up in large numbers, especially those 18 to 24. ，所以這篇文章不是關於紐約的 10 個小姐，而是有關年輕人吸菸的事情。Curtis 只是利用在酒吧裡的小姐來吸引我們讀這篇文章，賦予吸菸問題一些「人的面貌」。

以下只是個有趣的嘗試，把上述的文章改寫一下：

THE DANGERS OF SMOKING
By Scott Dreyer

Smoking is a very serious problem. It is especially serious for young adults in the 18 to 24 age range. One in five young women smokes. It has been a problem for many years. The problem does not seem to be going away! Perhaps it is the fault of the tobacco companies or Hollywood. Maybe women just want to stay thin! Thankfully, some young women are now trying to quit smoking. Keep reading this interesting article to find out how!

Do you want to keep reading this? No! And why not? It is boring. We have all read anti-smoking literature for years, and this is just one more (badly-written) example.

Here is a way to summarize "Start Strong" using a mathematical formula.

Catchy Title + Intriguing Hook + Clear Thesis Statement = A Great Start!

As you keep this formula in mind, I think you will be creating better, more attractive openings, to "hook" your reader. Remember: most readers decide within the *first few sentences* if they want to keep reading your material or not. Start strong!

Writers' block 寫作瓶頸

Before we go to Step 2, here is a word about Writers' Block: It is normal to think you have *nothing to say*! You stare at that blank page, or blank computer screen, ready to scream! You just DO NOT know how to start!

Take a deep breath, gentle reader: we have all been there. If you do not know how to start your paper, maybe try starting from the MIDDLE. In other words, imagine you want to write about the difficulty of learning a foreign language, or your first pet. If you cannot think of a great title or hook, just tell a story about how you first learned a foreign language, or something about your childhood pet. The actual story may be in the middle of the book, but just write something, and eventually, you will think of how to create an introduction.

久以來看過太多反菸的文章了，而這樣的寫法只不過又是老調重彈。

以下利用數學公式來為「有力的開始」這一節作個總結！

搶眼的題目＋引人興趣的切入點＋清楚的主旨句＝好的開始

只要把這公式謹記在心，你就能創作出更佳、更具吸引力的開頭來吸引讀者的注意力。切記：多數讀者看完前幾句就會決定是否要往下繼續讀，所以開場一定要有力！

在進入第二個步驟前，可以稍微談一下所謂的寫作瓶頸。寫不出東西來是很正常的事，你瞪著空白紙張或電腦螢幕，只想大聲尖叫，因為你根本不知道從何下筆。

親愛的讀者，先作個深呼吸。我們都經歷過相同的瓶頸。如果你不知道如何開頭，也許可以從中間開始寫。換句話說，假如你要撰寫學習外語的困難或是你的第一隻寵物，但你想不出一個很好的題目或切入點，就先從你如何開始學習外語、或你童年時寵物的往事開始寫起。這些故事是要放在文章的中間，但只要你持續寫些東西，你終究會想出來如何撰寫文章的開頭。

IN SUM 總結

Brainstorm to find a topic. Make an outline or web to organize your main points. Launch with a catchy title and hook to grab the reader's attention. Use a thesis statement and topic sentences to guide your reader.

腦力激盪出一個主題，擬定寫作大綱或網狀圖來組織你的重點，提出一個搶眼的題目和切入點來吸引讀者的注意。使用主旨句和主題句來引導你的讀者。

2 Use Strong Nouns
使用有力的名詞

Words—so innocent and powerless as they are, as standing in a dictionary, how potent for good and evil they become in the hands of one who knows how to combine them.

字詞在字典裡看來是如此單純和軟弱，但一到擅於結合字詞的作家手裡，就瞬間成為極度善良與邪惡的化身。

—Nathaniel Hawthorne, US author (1804-1864)

Nouns are like the building blocks of your writing. Just as your home would crumble if it were built of poor bricks, so too nouns can make or break your writing.

名詞好比是寫作中的建材，就像房屋若用劣質的磚頭建造就會崩塌，而名詞也一樣會讓你的作品堅實或是塌陷。

This is where a good vocabulary comes in. Think of <u>one strong noun</u> that can do the work of two or three weaklings.

好的詞彙用法就是以一個強有力的名詞來取代兩三個虛浮的字眼。

- The **small child** wobbled.   →   The toddler wobbled.
- Robert is an **extremely smart boy**.   →   Robert is a genius.
- Myrtle was **such a godly woman**.   →   Myrtle was a saint.
- Billy, your paper is a **true work of art**!   →   Billy, your paper is a masterpiece!
- Fincastle, Virginia is a quaint **little town**.   →   Fincastle, Virginia is a quaint hamlet.

Maybe you have noticed by now, and I do not want to sound too violent, but part of your job is to kill adjectives. In other words, <u>replace an adjective (or two) and a weak noun with one strong, specific noun</u>, i.e.:

你可能已經注意到，而且我實在不想形容得過於暴力，但寫作時有一部分的工作就是要消滅形容詞。換句話說，就是要用一個強有力的特定名詞來取代形容詞和虛空的名詞。例如：

- Rebecca ordered a **prime steak**. → Rebecca ordered a rib-eye.

- He drove an **expensive sports car**. → He drove a Jaguar.

- Turn right at the **small, wooden house**. → Turn right at the cabin.

- Wow, that girl is **really pretty**! → Wow, that girl is a beauty!

- The storm was **very destructive**. → The storm was a nightmare.

- Thanks for the dinner. It was **really delicious**. → Thanks for the dinner; it was a treat.

- She carried an **expensive designer** bag. → She carried a Gucci bag.

As you cut adjectives, try especially to get rid of weak adjectives like good, bad, nice, etc.

刪除形容詞時，特別要去除掉虛浮的形容詞例如 good, bad, nice 等。

IN SUM 總結

Use strong nouns to power-up your writing: "Coke" instead of "soft drink," "mansion" instead of "fancy big house," "brick ranch" instead of "one-story home made of brick," etc.

使用有力的名詞來強化文章：例如用 Coke 來取代 soft drink，用 mansion 代替 fancy big house，用 brick ranch 而不要用 one-story home made of brick 等。

■ Activity

3.3 Now you try some.
現在你來試試看。

1. The plates fell with a <u>loud noise</u>.

   → The plates fell with a/n _____.

2. We had a <u>large meal</u> at Thanksgiving!

   → We had a _____ at Thanksgiving!

3. Dad gave a dollar to the <u>poor man</u> on the corner.

   → Dad gave a dollar to the _____ on the corner.

4. A beautiful <u>glass lamp</u> hung over the dining room table.

   → A beautiful _____ hung over the dining room table.

3.4 Now think up a few sentences of your own. Create three with an adjective (or two) and a weak noun; then rewrite it with one strong noun. (Do not bother changing the verbs yet; just focus on adjectives and nouns.)
現在換你造幾個句子，首先寫出具有一兩個形容詞加上虛浮名詞的句子，再改寫成具有一個強有力名詞的句子。
（先不管動詞，只要更改形容詞和名詞即可。）

Example:

Dull: <u>We own a **small red tropical fish**</u>.

Better: <u>We own a **red beta**</u>.

1. Dull _____

   Better _____

2. Dull _____

   Better _____

3. Dull _____

Better _____

(Suggested answers are in the Answer Key on page 200.)

STEP 3 **Employ Vivid Verbs**
使用生動的動詞

If nouns are the building blocks of writing, verbs are the jet fuel because they propel your language. And as with nouns, avoid the common, dull verbs when you can; instead, employ vivid, colorful ones. In particular, cut *be* verbs (*am*, *is*, *was*, *will be*, etc.) when possible.

若把名詞喻為寫作的建材，那動詞就是噴射機的燃油，因為動詞可以驅動你的文字。而與使用名詞一樣，儘量避免使用平淡無奇的動詞，而改用生動富有色彩的動詞。特別盡可能少用 be 動詞（如 am, is, was, will be 等）。

- Emily **was** nervous before the interview. → Emily trembled and bit her nails before the interview.

- The car **came** to a halt. → The car screeched to a halt.

- "Are we there yet?" Meghan **asked**. → "Are we there yet?" Meghan whined.

- The lawnmower **made noises** and **stopped running**. → The lawnmower sputtered and died.

- "I hate this!" she **said unthinkingly**. → "I hate this!" she blurted out.

- Robbie **walked quickly** up the stairs to see his date. → Robbie sprinted up the stairs to see his date.

Verbs not only make your sentences stronger, but they tell the reader of the action. Look at how different verbs change the whole tone of these sentences.

動詞不僅讓你的句子更有力，也能告訴讀者文章中的動作。看看以下的句子，不同的動詞如何改變整句的語氣。

- The soldiers went up the mountain.

Boring, right? And we do not know how or why the soldiers "went up the mountain."

以上的句子很乏味，而且我們也不知道士兵為何以及如何 went up the mountain。

Now, have a look:

再看看下面的句子：

1. The soldiers trudged up the mountain.

2. The soldiers clawed their way up the mountain.

3. The soldiers inched their way up the mountain.

4. The soldiers fought their way up the mountain.

5. The soldiers charged up the mountain.

6. The soldiers advanced up the mountain.

Note how each sentence is different, depending on the *verb*. Numbers 1-4 imply the soldiers worked hard to climb the mountain, slowly, while 5 shows they moved quickly, and 6 is more vague.

因為使用不同的動詞，使每個句子的意義都不一樣。第一到第四句的動詞意謂士兵上山的過程既艱苦又漫長，第五句就感覺行動快多了，而第六句的意義則比較模糊。

Here are a few more:

以下還有更多例句：

1. "I am the fastest runner in my school," David said.

2. "I am the fastest runner in my school," David claimed.

3. "I am the fastest runner in my school," David boasted.

4. "I am the fastest runner in my school," David admitted.

5. "I am the fastest runner in my school," David blurted out.

Number 1 is neutral; 2 casts a doubt over what David says because a writer can use "claimed" to show skepticism; 3 shows pride; 4 shows humility; and 5 shows he spoke without thinking.

第一句是不具立場的，第二句顯示對 David 所說的話存疑，因為作者使用 claimed 來表示其懷疑的態度，第三句表現出自傲，第四句就顯示謙遜，而第五句則表示是未加思索、脫口而出。

Also, look for ways to turn nouns into verbs. For instance,

接著來看看把名詞轉為動詞的方法，例如：

- We watched the hawk **fly circles** in the sky. → We watched the hawk circle in the sky.

- We **had breakfast** at McDonald's. → We breakfasted at McDonald's.

- Quickly **take a shower** and go! → Quickly shower and go!

- First **take a rest** and then work later tonight. → First rest and then work later tonight.

<u>Cut weak helping verbs when possible.</u> This reduces your word number without losing any meaning.

盡可能刪除虛弱的助動詞，除了可精簡字數又不失原義。

| WEAK | The robot **can perform** properly on the website. |
| BETTER | The robot performs properly on the website. |

<u>Use strong verbs rather than awkward noun-verb combinations.</u>

使用有力的動詞，少用生硬的名詞－動詞組合字。

Found on a sign by a sink:

這是我在廚房水槽看到的標示：

| WEAK | "No Food Dumping" |
| BETTER | "Do not dump food in the sink" |

| WEAK | Computer Assessment model generation demands great effort. |
| BETTER | Generating computerized assessment models demands great effort. |

Now read these two sentences below, keeping in mind strong nouns and vivid verbs. Which sets the scene better?

現在閱讀以下兩個句子，注意有力的名詞和生動的動詞，哪一句把場景描述得較生動呢？

- The girl, eating her ice cream, sat on the deck under the shade tree.

- Sarah, savoring her raspberry sherbet, lounged on the deck under the maple.

You probably agree that the second sentence is *far* better. Why? With better nouns and verbs, it paints a better picture!

Maybe this chart will help you find more zippy verbs. (Just do not get carried away and always try to use confusing words, as Step 4 below explains. If the simplest verb is best, great, use it. But consider stronger verbs too.)

你可能也同意第二句較佳，為什麼呢？因為它用了較好的名詞和動詞，描繪出更佳的場景。

下表也許可以幫助你學習更多生動的動詞（但不要矯枉過正，老是用一些令人困惑的字，請見步驟四的說明。如果簡單的動詞就足以表情達意，那用它就好，只是也可考慮使用較強烈的動詞。）

Instead of this verb...	Maybe use this one
cry	weep, sob, tear up, burst into tears
drive	zip, speed, steer
eat	consume, wolf down, gobble, pick at, savor
go	set off, set out, travel, exit, take off
hit	strike, smack, thwack, ping, wallop
laugh	cackle, giggle, chuckle, roar, burst out
make	create, craft, design, invent, produce, manufacture
say	speak, declare, pronounce, state, exclaim
sleep	snooze, doze, slumber, drift off, fall into a trance, catnap, catch 40 winks
talk	chat, speak, discuss, confer
walk	saunter, stroll, hike, amble
want	desire, wish for, fancy, covet, hope for

work	labor, toil, exert, slave away
write	jot down, scribble, note, record, type

IN SUM 總結

Employ powerful verbs that set the scene and explain the action. Where possible, cut weak verbs like "walk," "go," "say," or the "be" verbs.

使用動態十足的動詞可以描繪場景並描述發生的事件。儘量少用薄弱的動詞如 walk, go, say, be 等字。

▪ **Activity**

3.5 Now you try some: Replace the boring verb with a zesty one.

現在換你來試試看，把無趣的動詞改得生動活潑一些。

1. The car drove down the Parkway. → The car _____ down the Parkway.

2. Victor ate his scrambled eggs. → Victor _____ his scrambled eggs.

3. The two old friends talked for hours. → The two old friends _____ for hours.

4. The toddler walked across the floor. → The toddler _____ across the floor.

3.6 Now, create a few sentences from scratch, first with a dull verb, then a vivid one.

先寫一句比較單調乏味的句子，再改寫成生動有力的句子。

1. Dull _____

   Better _____

2. Dull _____

   Better _____

3. Dull _____

   Better _____

(Suggested answers are in the Answer Key on page 201.)

4 Use Harold Words
使用簡單的字

I never write metropolis *for seven cents because I can get the same price for* city. *I never write* policeman *because I can get the same money for* cop.

我從不為了七分錢而用 metropolis 這個字，因為只要寫 city 就能賺到相同的錢。同理我也從不寫 policeman，只寫 cop。

—Mark Twain, American author and humorist
The Alphabet and Simplified Spelling speech, December 9, 1907
http://www.twainquotes.com/Word.html

To give you a short history lesson, 1066 was a key year in world history. That year, William the Conqueror of Normandy, France, invaded Britain and defeated the Anglo-Saxon king, Harold, at the Battle of Hastings. We call this event the Norman Conquest, and it transformed England and the English language. Before 1066, the Anglo-Saxon language of England was basically a type of German. However, when William's Normans invaded England, they introduced many French-based words, where they have remained since. In countless ways, these words have enriched and beautified the English language, especially in fields of art, law, and food, and also helped give English the world's largest vocabulary. For example, our word *pork* comes from the French *porc*, and that is good, because if we took our word from the German word *Schweinefleisch*, we may have had to call pork *swine flesh*, which does not sound very appetizing. Likewise, our words such as *beef, venison, poultry*, etc. come from French.

我們先上一下歷史課，1066 年是世界史上的關鍵年。當年，法國諾曼第征服者威廉入侵英國，並在哈斯汀戰場擊潰盎格魯撒克遜人的國王哈洛。我們稱這個事件為諾曼征服，它從此改變了英國和英文。在 1066 年之前，英國的盎格魯撒克遜語言基本上是一種德文，但是威廉所率領的諾曼人入侵英國後引進了許多法文字，從此就變成英文的一部分。這些法文在眾多層面上豐富美化了英文，尤其是在藝術、法律和食物等領域，並使得英文成為全世界字彙最多的語言。例如英文的 pork 就來自法文的 porc，這是件好事，因為如果用了德文的 Schweinefleisch，那我們可能就必須稱 pork 為 swine flesh，聽起來實在不怎麼美味。同樣的，我們現在使用的字如 beef, venison, poultry 也都是來自法文。

However, just as these words can beautify the English language, some have a disadvantage: they can be very long, whereas words with Anglo-Saxon roots tend to be shorter. You may have the impression from school that the longer the word, the better. But that is not always so. Often, shorter words have more punch, letting the writer say more, quicker. I read somewhere that Lincoln's Second Inaugural Address held only 701 words, of which *505 had only one syllable*, and 122 had only two.

Lincoln was a master of saying much with few words, and we can all learn from him.

One wise guy put it this way: *"Never use a long word when a diminutive one will suffice."*[4] So, try to keep it simple, or as my wife sometimes says, "KISS: Keep It Simple, Sweetheart." In your writing, rather than *discontinue*, use *stop*; instead of *momentarily*, say *soon*, etc.

"Now wait," you may be thinking. "Doesn't this step contradict steps 2 and 3, Use Strong Nouns and Verbs?" Actually, no. Use strong words, and avoid unnecessarily long ones. For example, "stroll" is a strong word to replace "walk," while "perambulate" is probably not, because it is needlessly long. Keep in mind <u>syllable</u> count, as well as <u>word</u> count.

To illustrate, and to have a little fun, here are the names of two Christmas carols...but in confusing English!

然而這些字雖然美化了英文，但也帶來一些缺點：這些字通常比較長，而帶有盎格魯撒克遜字根的字則通常較短。你在課堂上所得的印象可能覺得愈長的字愈有學問，但事實上並不見得，通常較短的字反而充滿活力，讓作者表達得更多、更快速。我在某處看過說林肯的第二任就職演講稿僅有 701 個字，而且其中的 505 個字都是單音節，而 122 個字是雙音節。

林肯是以少數字詞即可表達豐富義涵的大師，我們可以跟他學習。

有位自以為聰明的人曾這樣說：「凡是用簡單明瞭扼要的簡短字詞就足以表達的情況時就不要用長字。」[4] 所以文字儘量精簡，或像我太太有時說的：「KISS: Keep Simple, Sweetheart.」寫作時，若要用 discontinue，則不如用 stop；要用 momentarily，則不如用 soon 等。注意諸如此類的用法。

你也許會心想：「等一下！這個步驟不是和第二、第三步驟的使用生動有力名詞和動詞相互矛盾嗎？」其實不然。我們要使用有力的字詞並避免不必要的長字，例如 stroll 是個生動的字，可以取代 walk，但像 perambulate 可能就不太好，因為它是不必要的長字。記住，音節數和字數都要注意。

為了進一步闡明和好玩起見，以下以兩首聖誕歌曲的名稱為例，左邊是令人困惑的英文，而右邊才是眞

---

4 此句諷刺之處在於這句英文中的 diminutive 和 suffice 就是長字，而不是短字，因此譯文也特意拉長為囉唆的冗詞。比較簡潔的說法為 "Never use a long word when a short one will do."，可譯為「足以用短字表達之處就不用長字。」

Next to them are the real names. You can see the need to keep it simple!

正的歌名，你就可以看出簡單表達的必要性。

Complicated Name	Real Name
Five p.m. to six a.m. without noise	Silent Night
Exuberance directed to the planet	Joy to the World

IN SUM 總結

Do not use long words just for their own sake. If a longer word is the best choice, great, use it; but otherwise, KISS.

不要為了使用長字而用它。如果長字是最佳的選擇，那也很好，否則的話還是以簡短為原則。

Activity

3.7 Now rewrite these, in layman's terms, and try to keep the original meaning, but with as few words and syllables as possible.

用平常的方式，試著以盡可能較少的字數和音節重寫以下的句子，但要維持原有的意義。

1. We regret to inform you that we are unable to provide assistance at this present moment. (By the way, how many syllables does this monster have? _____)

_____

2. The hot atmospheric conditions were oppressive.

_____

(Suggested answers are in the Answer Key on page 202.)

5 Use Some Glue
使用黏著劑

Let us review. So far, we have learned about how to 1. Start Strong, 2. Use Strong Nouns, 3. Employ Vivid Verbs, and 4. Use Harold (i.e. when possible, simple) Words. If you have noticed, most of these steps are about *single words*, or *small groups of words*. This fifth step, Use Some Glue, now focuses on your writing *as a whole*. To return to the building metaphor, we learned that words are like the bricks we use to build a house. Imagine a home of loose bricks: it would soon wobble and fall! The bricks are held together with mortar, so that the bricks gradually rise to create a whole wall, and eventually a building.

我們先回顧一下，目前我們已學過：1. 有力的開始、2. 使用有力的名詞、3. 使用生動的動詞和 4. 使用簡單的字。如果你有注意到，這些步驟大多探討個別的單字或字群。而第五個步驟的使用黏著劑，則是進而把文章視為一個整體。再回到蓋房子的比喻，我們知道字詞就好像是蓋房子所需的磚塊，如果磚塊結構鬆散，房子很快就會搖晃倒塌。磚塊若是用灰泥漿砌合在一起，讓磚塊逐漸堆疊成一堵牆，最後終可蓋好一棟房屋。

It is the same with words. Just as mortar holds bricks together, so "glue," or transitions and structure, hold your words together to make a unified paper.

用字也是如此。如同灰泥漿把磚塊固定在一起，「黏著劑」或者稱轉折語和結構，也能銜接你的字詞，構成一篇完整的文章。

Topic sentence 主題句

One important part of "glue" is a topic sentence. Do you remember back in Step 1, when we learned about a thesis statement? (That is one sentence that contains the main idea of your writing.) In fact, topic sentences and thesis statements are quite similar. Just as a thesis statement is the main idea for your paper, the topic sentence is the main idea for *one paragraph*. And to be clear, each paragraph should have one topic sentence. Read the two paragraphs below and see if you can find the two topic sentences.

其中一種重要的「黏著劑」是主題句，還記得我們在第一個步驟學過主旨句嗎？（也就是點出文章主要重點的句子。）實際上主題句和主旨句相當類似，只是主旨句是整篇文章的重點，而主題句是一個段落的重點。為了使文章清楚，每一段都應該要有一句主題句。閱讀以下兩段文字，看看你是否能找到它們的主題句。

Jealousy is a big problem for many people. For one thing, it is widespread; probably everyone has struggled with it at one time or another. Second, it can damage relationships. When we are jealous of someone, we tend not to like him or her, although our bad feelings usually do not hurt the other person's success. Third, when we are jealous of others, we tend to overlook what we already have, and therefore do not enjoy or use the blessings that we already have.

Overcoming jealousy is not easy, but it is possible. How? As with overcoming all problems, the first step is to admit the problem. Recognize the jealousy and decide to combat it. Second, try to enjoy and learn from other people's successes. If we look at other people as potential teachers instead of a competitor, it may give us a better attitude. Finally, when we look around and appreciate what we already have, and try to build on that, we may find we can overcome the power of jealousy in our lives!

Did you find the two topic sentences? In the first paragraph, the topic sentence was "Jealousy is a big problem for many people." In the second, it was "Overcoming jealousy is not easy, but it is possible." Note how the topic sentence is clear, and it sets the direction for the rest of the paragraph. It lets the reader know where you are going. Also, note where the topic sentences were: <u>at the beginning of each paragraph</u>. This placement is not essential, but the first sentence is *often* the best place for the topic sentence.

Now, underline the topic sentences in the following paragraphs.

你找到兩句主題句了嗎？第一段的主題句是 Jealousy is a big problem for many people.；而第二段的主題句是 Overcoming jealousy is not easy, but it is possible.。有沒有注意到這些主題句很清楚，指引出這段文章的脈絡，讓讀者掌握得到作者的想法。同時注意這兩句主題句的位置是在每一段的開頭。這個位置並不是絕對的，但通常第一句是主題句的最佳所在地。

在以下的段落中找出主題句並畫底線。

I will always remember my first year in Taiwan. Being so far away from home was scary...but also exciting. Learning Chinese was tough, but everyone was so positive and encouraging. "You speak Chinese very well!" they would enthuse after I would haltingly order a bowl of noodles or ask where the bathroom was. Getting around town was a challenge at first because I was terrified on the scooter and most of the roads seemed to be at weird angles. And having all the road signs in Chinese did not make things any easier.

Gradually, though, I got used to life in Asia. My Chinese advanced to where I could ask simple directions, understand simple stories, and even make a few little jokes! Over time, the traffic seemed less mystifying and I began to get a handle on some of the major roads and even shortcuts. I got used to the food, made friends, and began to understand a little of the culture. That first Chinese New Year was especially fun, because I was invited to celebrate the night with a Chinese family.

After just ten months, Taiwan was beginning to feel like home! I had succeeded on my first job and had been hired at new one, had a circle of friends, had stayed healthy, and was able to have more complex conversations in Chinese. Adopting a dog off the street, *Shao Huang*, also helped me feel like less of an outsider and more of a true member of the community. I will always thank God for that first year in Taiwan.

How did you do? The three topic sentences are the following:　　　　　　　　　　　　　　　找到了嗎？三個主題句分別如下：

1. I will always remember my first year in Taiwan.
   (This is also the thesis statement—and the hook—for the entire article.)

2. Gradually, though, I got used to life in Asia.

3. After just ten months, Taiwan was beginning to feel like home!

Did you see how each topic sentence sets the stage, or shows the direction, of its paragraph? The rest of the paragraph merely explains the original point. Did you also notice that these three topic sentences were also the first sentence of each paragraph? That will not always be the case, but it often is. You may wonder about the last sentence: "I will always thank God for that first year in Taiwan." It may look like a topic sentence, but it is not. It is simply the conclusion, designed to echo and emphasize the thesis statement and first topic sentence: "I will always remember my first year in Taiwan."

Now try this. Below are paragraphs from a *Reader's Digest* article...with the topic sentences missing. Read the paragraphs and pick the best topic sentence (A, B, or C) from the options below.

你看出主題句都能爲每一段文字設定背景或指示方向了嗎？該段落的其他文字只是用來解釋原有的重點。你有沒有注意到這三句主題句也都是每一段的第一個句子？雖然寫作上不一定都是如此，但通常還是放在最前面。你或許會覺得最後一個句子 I will always thank God for that first year in Taiwan. 看起來很像是主題句，但它其實不是。它只是個結語，用來呼應及強調同時是主旨句和主題句的 I will always remember my first year in Taiwan. 。

現在換你來試試，以下是從《讀者文摘》上節錄的段落，可是缺乏主題句。請你讀完後從下面的選項 (A, B, C) 中選出最佳的主題句：

1. _____

For many of us, it's a flashy Wall Street banker type who flies a private jet, collects cars and lives the kind of decadent lifestyle that would make Donald Trump proud.

A. According to one survey, there are more millionaires alive today than ever before.

B. When you think of "millionaire," what image comes to mind?

C. Have you ever wished you could become a millionaire?

2. _____

What motivates them isn't material possessions but the choices that money can bring: "For the rich, it's not about getting more stuff. It's about having the freedom to make almost any decision you want," says T. Harv Eker, author of *Secrets of the Millionaire Mind*. Wealth means you can send your child to any school or quit a job you don't like.[5]

5 Lewis, Kristyn Kusek. *Reader's Digest*. "Secrets of Self-Made Millionaires." December 2007, pp. 141-145.

A. Why are there more millionaires today than ever before?

B. Most millionaires do not have exciting lives.

C. But many modern millionaires live in middle-class neighborhoods, work full-time and shop in discount stores like the rest of us.

For paragraph 1, the topic sentence was B and for 2 it was C. Look again at #1: the paragraph implies that rich people have fancy lives, so the topic sentence is the question, asking what we expect from the wealthy. For #2, the paragraph explains that most wealthy do not want to just buy more stuff, so the topic sentence explains that most millionaires have quite "normal" lives.

第一段的主題句是 B，第二段是 C。再看一次第一題，該段暗示有錢人享有富裕的生活，所以主題句是個問句，問我們對有錢人的印象是什麼。至於第二題，它解釋最富有的人並不見得想要購買更多的東西，所以主題句說明多數的百萬富翁其實是過著相當「正常」的生活。

Activity

3.8 Here are some sample topic sentences. Now, write a paragraph to match the topic sentence.

根據以下這些主題句來寫成一個段落。

1. If I had one free week and NT$30,000, I would go to my favorite spot in Taiwan for a vacation.

_____

_____

_____

_____

_____

2. There are many qualities one looks for in a friend, but three characteristics stand out.

_____

_____

_____

_____

_____

(Suggested answers are in the Answer Key on page 203.)

Transitions 轉折語

To review, "using glue" is basically arranging your words so that they "stick" together well. One big part of that is the topic sentence, which helps each paragraph hold together. Another part of "glue" is using transitions. Transitions are words that show the reader which direction the writer is taking. There are many ways to do this. As we learned earlier, with the Comparison-Contrast, transitions can indicate similarities or differences.

現在來複習一下：使用「黏著劑」基本上是來安排你的字詞，讓它們緊密連結在一起。其中一個要素是主題句，可讓整個段落附著在一塊。另一種「黏著劑」是使用轉折語。轉折語指引讀者遵循作者前進的方向。轉折語的功用很多，在我們之前學過的比較對照類的文章中，轉折語就可指出類似或差異之處。

Transitions that show the same direction 顯示相同方向的轉折語

- and
- also
- in addition
- furthermore
- additionally
- likewise
- as well
- too
- besides
- moreover

Transitions that show different direction 顯示不同方向的轉折語

- in contrast
- but
- however
- despite
- though
- although
- even though
- nevertheless
- nonetheless
- yet
- conversely
- while
- on the other hand

Transitions that show relationships 顯示關係的轉折語

- because
- since
- therefore
- hence
- so
- thus
- consequently
- accordingly
- that is why

Transitions that show time or importance 顯示時間或重要性的轉折語

These are some of my favorites. If you are writing about an historical event or anything that involves time order, make it clear to the reader what happened first, then second, next, finally, etc. The same is true if

以下是我喜歡用的一些轉折語。如果你要寫一個歷史事件或任何牽涉到時間順序的主題，一定要清楚讓讀者知道什麼是最先、然後第二、接下來、最後發生什麼事。同樣

you are writing items of importance, or components of something.

地，若你要撰寫某些項目的重要性或某物的組成成分，都可以使用相同的技巧。

- first
- next
- second
- third
- fourth
- before
- soon
- later
- finally
- especially

Here is a fine example of how one student used "glue" to make a paper that is short but clear. Her topic sentence states her case: she will focus on three traits of Judaism. The last sentence wraps up powerfully. Judaism, despite its small number of followers, has had a huge impact on world history. Note also how Emily uses number words ("first," "secondly," and "finally") to make her points clear and lead her reader step by step.

以下是篇很好的範例，說明一名學生如何使用「黏著劑」使這篇文章雖然簡短，卻相當清楚。她的主題句說出了她的用意：她將探討猶太教的三個特色。而最後一句作了強而有力的結束：儘管猶太教的信徒人數不多，但是對世界歷史的影響很大。注意 Emily 如何使用數量詞 (first, secondly, finally) 來清楚表達意見並一步步引領讀者閱讀。

Judaism

Emily C.

Judaism focuses on three central themes, which set it distinctively apart from other religions. First, it is important to understand that Judaism is a monotheistic religion: Jews worship one, and only one, all-powerful God. Secondly, the Jewish Bible places great emphasis on the covenant between God and Abraham, in which God promises to bless Abraham and his descendants in return for Abraham's absolute faith. Finally, the Jewish Bible recognizes mankind's strong tendency to sin, and God's forgiveness of that sin. In conclusion, while the Jewish people are comparatively small in number, their influence across the globe has been enormous: this is a religion that has truly changed the world.

Notice how the above paragraph is short, yet clear. The transition words—*first, second, finally*—move the flow.

Note below how a few transition words not only help the flow, but also can help to combine several choppy sentences into fewer, smoother ones.

這個段落雖短，但很清楚。使用轉折語如 first, second, finally 來推動文意。

看看以下這些轉折語如何讓文字更流暢，並把零散的句子組合成較平順的句子。

CHOPPY	The phone rang. Ya-ting did not hear it. She was outside.
BETTER	The phone rang, but Ya-ting did not hear it because she was outside. (**Different direction & relationships**)
CHOPPY	It was raining outside. We let the cat in.
BETTER	It was raining outside so we let the cat in. (**Relationships**)
CHOPPY	Taipei is large. Hong Kong is large.
BETTER	Taipei and Hong Kong are both large. (**Same direction**)
CHOPPY	It was raining. We went on our trip.
BETTER	It was raining; however, we still went on our trip. (**Different direction**)

Activity

3.9 Below is a paragraph about Chinese history with some transition words missing. This story involves issues of both chronology and importance. See which words from the word bank fit the blanks. You will use each word once. (Hint: use the number words—first, second, third—for blanks 2, 4, and 7.)

以下這段有關中國歷史的文章缺少了一些轉折語，這篇文章同時牽涉到時間性和重要性。從字庫中選擇恰當的字填入空格，一個字只能使用一次。（提示：在空格 2, 4, 7 中要使用數量詞 first, second, third）

Word Bank:

first	second	third	when	lastly
and	yet	during	under	however

Early 20th Century China

The early part of the twentieth-century was an important 1.＿＿＿＿＿＿＿ bloody and confusing time for China. 2.＿＿＿＿＿＿＿, in 1911, a popular revolution overthrew the last dynasty. China established its first republic under Sun Yat-sen and seemed to be modernizing. 3.＿＿＿＿＿＿＿, violence and confusion soon followed.

4.＿＿＿＿＿＿＿, Civil War broke out between the Nationalist forces led by Chiang Kai-shek 5.＿＿＿＿＿＿ the Communist forces 6.＿＿＿＿＿＿ Mao Zedong.

7.＿＿＿＿＿＿＿, in the 1930s, more violence erupted when Japan invaded in WW II. China suffered greatly 8.＿＿＿＿＿＿ the Second World War. 9.＿＿＿＿＿＿＿ Japan surrendered in 1945, the Chinese Civil War between the Nationalists and Communists erupted again. 10.＿＿＿＿＿＿, Mao Zedong proclaimed the formation of the People's Republic of China in 1949, and Mainland China has had a Communist government ever since.

(Answers are in the Answer Key on page 203.)

Bouncing 彈跳

Here is one more trick that top writers and speakers use to "glue" their presentations together: <u>bouncing</u>. "Bouncing" is simply stating a fact or principle, *then giving a story, joke, or example to illustrate the principle*. Or, you can first tell the story or example, then cite the principle. Why? People usually forget the dry, abstract rule you teach...but they will remember the illustrative story or example. And if they remember the story—presto!—they will probably remember the idea *behind* it.

另外還有一種頂尖作家和演說家所用的「黏著劑」技巧:「彈跳」,也就是陳述一件事實或原則後,再跳到一個故事、笑話或例子來說明該原則。或者也可以先講故事或例子之後再引述該原則。為什麼要這樣做呢?人們容易遺忘枯燥抽象的規範,但他們會記得用來作說明的故事或例子。如果他們能記得故事,他們當然也會記得故事背後的道理。

For instance, I teach high school, and there are many ideas I want to share with my students: *work hard, be in school daily, overcome hardship, do your best.* These are messages that adults try to share with young people anywhere, but they are dry, abstract facts! And many kids have heard these messages so much that they ignore them.

例如我現在在教高中生,我有很多想法想跟學生分享,例如努力用功、每天到校、克服困難、竭盡全力等。大人有許多訊息想跟年輕人分享,但是這些訊息是枯燥抽象的事情,很多孩子已經聽過太多遍了,容易忽略這些訊息。

This semester I had a student, Robert, who was plagued by great hardship. First he lost his grandmother, and then his family had a house fire and lost everything. However, this student kept coming to school...*and his grades in all his classes went up!* When I asked him why he was now more successful in school, he said, "I think I used to take things for granted, expecting life to continue on as it always had. But after the fire I learned to appreciate things and I also learned that, if I have a good education, I can always replace anything I lose."

這學期我有個學生 Robert 遭逢巨變。先是他的祖母去世,接著家裡的房子遭受祝融之災,所有東西化為烏有。然而 Robert 仍持續上學,成績也愈來愈好。當我問他為何現在在校的表現反而比以前好,他說:「我以前把一切都視為理所當然,覺得生活會像往常一樣持續下去。但家中遭遇火災後,我學習到要對所有的事情感恩,我也體會到如果我有良好的教育,就能再得到我所失去的東西。」

Now, when I urge my students to attend school regularly and work hard, I tell them this story. "If anyone had an excuse to feel sorry for himself and stop doing schoolwork, it was Robert," I say. Once after I told this story a boy came up to me, confessing: "I have been getting lazy but now I realize I need to get serious about my schoolwork and grades, if I am ever going to get into the college I like." When I asked him why he had decided to get focused, he told me, "Hearing Robert's story."

See how it works? People may forget or even ignore your principle, but everyone loves a good story, and a story or practical example can often get past people's defenses and make an emotional impact, and this is what lasts.

And did you notice what just happened? To explain the concept of bouncing—a dry idea—I used Robert's story to illustrate it. In other words, I used bouncing to give you an example of bouncing. So just remember Robert's story, and you too can use bouncing to give your papers and speeches more power.

Rule of Three 三的原則

One final idea for this section is called the <u>Rule of Three</u>. When you are preparing an article or speech, three is a good number of points to make. One point is too weak, while nine or ten is probably too many to remember. Many preachers are trained to give the "three-point sermon," a talk with three main points

現在每當我想鼓勵學生每日到校和努力用功時，我都會告訴他們這個故事。我常說：「有任何藉口可以自怨自艾而不想寫功課的人，只有 Robert。」有一次我講完故事後，一名男同學跟我坦承：「我一直都很懶散，但現在我才明白，如果我想進理想中的大學，我需要更加努力讀書。」我問他為什麼現在決定要專注讀書了，他告訴我：「就是因為聽了 Robert 的故事。」

你看得出這其中的道理嗎？人們會忘記或甚至忽略你說的原則，但每個人都喜歡好聽的故事，而故事或實際的案例通常可以降低人們的防衛心理而對其情感造成衝擊，並記在腦海裡。

你有注意到嗎？剛剛所說的就是要解釋「彈跳」的概念，透過 Robert 的故事來說明原本枯燥的想法。換句話說，我利用「彈跳」來提供「彈跳」的例子。所以只要記得 Robert 的故事，你也可以使用「彈跳」來使你的文章或演說更具感染力。

本節最後要講的是「三的原則」，當你準備寫文章或演講時，將重點分成三點是很好的做法。只有一個重點的話太薄弱，而有九或十個重點又太多，無法讓人記住。許多受過訓練的牧師都是講「三個重點的佈道」，講詞中只有三個重點讓聽眾思考。也許你也注意到本書區分為三個主要

that the people are to consider. Perhaps you noticed that this book is divided into three main sections. So when you are thinking about arranging your essay or speech, or wondering how many examples to cite, you may want to follow the Rule of Three.

章節。所以當你思考要如何安排你的文章或演講，或是不知道要引述幾個案例時，不妨遵循「三的原則」。

IN SUM 總結

Use some Glue to make your ideas stick together. Use strong topic sentences to show the idea for each paragraph. Include transition words (first, however, on the other hand) to show relationships. And "bounce" between dry concepts and practical examples, to make the abstract ideas stick in your readers' minds.

使用「黏著劑」把所有的想法凝聚在一起。使用有力的主題句來表達每個段落的重點。包括使用轉折語 (first, however, on the other hand) 來呈現彼此間的關係。最後在枯燥的概念和實際例子之間「彈跳」，讓讀者在心中記住這些抽象的概念。

STEP 6 Cut Clutter
刪除冗詞

This step is related to the above steps: look for ways to say *more*, with *fewer words*. This is called "economy of language." An economical car does not use much gas; economical writing does not use many words. From school or elsewhere you may think that the more words you use, the better, but the main point is <u>quality</u> and not quantity.

此步驟與前述步驟都有關,是以較少的字詞表達更多的義涵,也就是所謂「言簡意賅」。如同省油的車不會耗費汽油,精簡的文章也不會使用太多的字。你從學校或其他地方所得的經驗可能會認為寫得愈多愈好,但最重要的是品質而非數量。

We live in an Age of Clutter. Our homes are often cluttered with junk mail, paperwork, unread magazines. We turn on our computers and find them cluttered too, with emails and spy ware. Our schedules may be cluttered with too many commitments. And our writing may be cluttered with unneeded words. Government writing, or "legalese," is especially notorious for this! Ask your parents to show you the government's tax catalogue.

我們生活在一個混亂的時代,家裡面總是堆滿垃圾郵件、文件、尚未翻閱的雜誌。打開電腦也是一團亂,充斥著大量電子郵件和間諜軟體。我們的時間表因太多承諾要做的事情而亂成一團。我們的寫作也會因使用不必要的字而混亂。政府出版品或「公文體」就是因冗詞而惡名昭彰,請爸媽給你看一下政府的申報繳稅說明就知道了。

Let us do some pruning. Cut these shabby phrases:

現在我們來修剪以下這些冗長的片語:

- at this point in time   →   now
- consequently   →   so
- more specifically   →   for example
- on the grounds that   →   because, since

As with the noun and verb practice earlier, try to cut *several words* in favor of *one strong word*.

仿照剛學過的名詞與動詞規則,將一連串的字用一個強有力的字代替。

- He stared at the **dark blue** sea. → He stared at the cobalt sea.
- The marble was a beautiful **blue-green color**. → The marble was a beautiful turquoise.
- This cake tastes **very good**. → This cake tastes delicious.
- We end class **in the neighborhood of** 4:00. → We end class about 4:00.

Here are a few examples my students created:

以下是我的學生所寫的例子：

- Joe **goes swimming** every morning. → Joe swims every morning.
- Please **use the mop to clean** the floor. → Please mop the floor.
- The dog **made loud noises**. → The dog barked.
- The **sun's beams of light** fell on me. → The sunshine fell on me.

The Art of Readable Writing contrasts two books on chess[6]. Which has more clutter? Which is catchier?

《The Art of Readable Writing》這本書中對照兩本討論西洋棋的書，哪一本比較囉嗦？哪一本又比較吸引人呢？

The Principles of Chess	*Learn Chess Fast!*
The pawn is the weakest, but not the least interesting, of all the forces. Its line of movement is forward only, or in one direction in file, one square at a time, save at its first time of moving, when it may advance one square or two squares at the option of the player—if he then has an option in the matter.	The pawn is paradoxical. Although it is the weakest of all the chessmen, it plays a vital role at all the stages of the game. The beginner despises the pawn for its weakness, but the chess-master fully appreciates its important qualities.

6 Flesh, Rudolf. *The Art of Readable Writing.* New York: Macmillan Publishing Company, 1949. p. 121.

If you think about it, you can usually cut a few words without losing any meaning. For example, in this book's rough draft, I wrote the following sentence three times.

如果你仔細思考一下，你通常可以刪除幾個字而不失去原有的意義。例如我在撰寫這本書的初稿時，光以下這句話就寫了三遍。

- The semi-colon is used to do several things. (8 words)

- The semi-colon can do several things. (6 words)

- The semi-colon does several things. (5 words)

IN SUM 總結

Try to say more with less.
表達言簡意賅。

Your ATTITUDE more than your APTITUDE determines your ALTITUDE.

是你的態度，而不是能力，來決定你高度。

–Zig Ziglar

Activity

3.10 **Now you try some.**

現在你來練習一下。

1. "Turn down the radio volume," Mom asked.

→ "_____," Mom asked.

2. You are requested to remain seated.

→ _____

3. "Stop it, David!" Harmony commanded in a loud voice.

→ "Stop it, David!" Harmony _____.

3.11 **Now, you create some sentences, first with clutter; then clean them up.**

請先造出冗贅的句子，再改寫成精簡的句子。

1. Cluttered _____

   Uncluttered _____

2. Cluttered _____

   Uncluttered _____

3. Cluttered _____

   Uncluttered _____

(Suggested answers are in the Answer Key on page 204.)

7 Practice Parallelism
練習平行結構

Often overlooked, this step can make your writing smoother, clearer, and shorter. Just as the rails of a train track must be parallel, try to make your structures parallel by expressing similar ideas in a sentence with similar grammatical forms.

此步驟經常被忽略,但它可以讓你的寫作更加流暢、清楚和簡短。就像火車的軌道必須平行,你也可使用文法形式近似的句子來表達類似的想法,讓你的結構也能夠平行。

Which sentence is clearer?

哪個句子比較清楚?

A. Taipei is very large; it has lots of people, and I find Taipei fascinating.

B. Taipei is large, crowded, and fascinating.

"B" is better, clearer, and less cluttered. Why? *Large, crowded,* and *fascinating* are all adjectives, in parallel structure.

B 句較佳,因為它比較清楚和精簡。為什麼呢?因為 large, crowded 和 fascinating 都是形容詞,形成平行的結構。

Here are some easy tips to remember. (For each set, the first sentence is not parallel, while the second one is.)

以下是一些平行結構的簡單訣竅。(每組的第一個句子不是平行的,第二句才是。)

1. Make adjectives parallel. 使形容詞平行

- The large dog snarled loudly and scared us.

  → The large, scary dog snarled at us.

2. Make nouns parallel. 使名詞平行

- Please bring charcoal, a box of matches, some meat dishes, and some kind of vegetable to the picnic. And we will need something to drink too.

  → Please bring charcoal, matches, meat, vegetables, and drinks to the picnic.

3. Make verbs parallel. 使動詞平行

- Victor, smiling, said "hello," then quickly bounded away.

    → Victor smiled, said "hello," then bounded away.
    (Notice the parallel verbs are all in the past tense.) （所有動詞在平行結構中皆為過去式。）

- My morning routine, after waking up, is to have some breakfast, and after having brushed my teeth, I try to leave home by 7:00.

    → My morning routine is to wake up, eat breakfast, brush my teeth, and leave home by 7:00.
    (These parallel verbs are all in the present tense.) （所有動詞在平行結構中皆為現在式。）

4. Make adverbs parallel. 使副詞平行

- He drove the car with great care and also safely.

    → He drove the car carefully and safely.

5. Make phrases, clauses, and comparisons parallel. 使片語、子句和比較平行

- Deborah is good with art as well as in the area of music.

    → Deborah is good with art as well as with music.

Here is an example from technical English, reporting on robot technology.

以下是科技英文的例句，報導機器人技術。

- Recently, this technology has been gradually adopted in industry, medical purposes, business and family applications.

    → Recently, this technology has been gradually adopted in industrial, medical, business, and family applications.
    (Make "industrial" an adjective and cut "purposes.")
    （用形容詞 industrial，並刪除 purposes。）

■ Activity

3.12 Make these sentences parallel.
將以下的句子改為平行結構。

1. To learn a foreign language is about as difficult as learning to play a musical instrument.

_____

2. Learning a foreign language requires work, an attitude of dedication, and one must also show a willingness to be self-disciplined.

_____

3. Three reasons why Kenting is such a popular resort are the beautiful scenery, the climate is usually warm, and many people find the outdoor activities to be very fun.

_____

(Suggested answers are in the Answer Key on page 205.)

8 Produce Powerful Punctuation
使用有效的標點

Not wanting to bore you with third grade grammar, we will skip discussing the period and comma and such; besides, there are grammar books far more complete than this if you need a big review. For this part, however, we will study a few lesser-used punctuation marks.

我不想拿（美國）小學三年級的文法來讓你覺得無聊，我們會略過句號和逗號的討論。再說，如果你需要複習，市面上很多文法書有更完整的說明。在這裡我們只探討一些較少用到的標點符號。

But first, to convince you of the importance of punctuation, here's a gem that Mike Riley, former editor of the *Roanoke Times*, showed my students recently:

首先，要先讓你知道標點符號的重要性，以下是《Roanoke Times》前任編輯最近給我的學生所看的佳例：

- A woman without her man is nothing.

What does this mean? Can you add any punctuation to change the sense?

這句話是什麼意思呢？你能加上標點來改變它的意義嗎？

As it now reads, it is very sexist: A woman without a man is a zero. However, now look:

目前的句子讀起來是有性別歧視的：沒有男人的女性就不是東西，但是再看：

- A woman: without her, man is nothing.

See? The words are the exact same, but by adding punctuation, you change the meaning entirely. It now means, a man without his woman is a zero.

看到了嗎？一樣的字，但加了標點後意思就完全改觀，現在變成沒有女人的男性就不是東西了。

Grammar is not known to be very funny, but you may like this joke.

大家都知道文法不是很有趣，但你可能會喜歡以下這則笑話：

A panda bear walks into a bar, orders a sandwich, and eats it. But when he's finished, he takes out a gun, kills the waiter, and heads toward the door. The bartender yells at him: "Hey! You just shot my waiter, and you didn't even pay for the sandwich!"

The panda looks over his shoulder and replies, "I'm a panda. Look it up in the dictionary."

The bartender then pulls out his dictionary and looks up "panda." He finds "Panda, (noun). An Asian mammal marked by distinctive black and white markings. Eats shoots and leaves."

"Eats shoots and leaves" means the panda eats bamboo shoots and leaves. However, with commas, it becomes: "eats, shoots, and leaves," thus explaining why he ate lunch, shot the man, then left. There is a clever grammar book by this title, *Eats Shoots and Leaves*, by Lynne Truss.

Eats shoots and leaves 意指熊貓「吃竹子的嫩枝和葉子」，但是加了逗號後就變成 eats, shoots, and leaves。這樣就可以解釋為何熊貓吃完午餐、開槍射人、然後離開。《Eats Shoots and Leaves》是 Lynne Truss 所著的一本有趣的文法書書名。

The colon (:) 冒號
This mark does several things.

它有幾個功能：

1. It can introduce an idea, list, or surprise. 它可引介想法、項目或令人驚訝的事物

- Victor had a choice to make: climb a tree or play with the cat.

- Bring these to class daily: your book, notebook, a pen or pencil, and a great attitude.

- After more than a week on the road, we finally saw it: Niagara Falls!

Activity

3.13 Add a colon to the following sentences.
在以下句子中加入冒號。

1. Its strong winds give Hsinchu its nickname The Windy City.

2. After years of planning and hard work, it had arrived graduation day!

3. Please bring these items to the picnic paper plates, cups, ice, and sandwiches.

3.14 Now, you write three sentences using a colon to introduce a list, idea, or surprise:
現在換你寫出使用冒號的三個句子，分別引介想法、項目或令人驚訝的事物。

1. _____

2. _____

3. _____

(Suggested answers are in the Answer Key on page 205.)

2. The colon can introduce a long quotation. (Introduce <u>shorter</u> quotations with a comma.) 冒號可引介長的引文（短的引文用逗號來引介）

- Thomas Jefferson began the Declaration of Independence thus: "When in the Course of human events, it becomes necessary for one people to dissolve the political bands which have connected them with another, and to assume among the powers of the earth, the separate and equal station to which the Laws of Nature and of Nature's God entitle them, a decent respect to the opinions of mankind requires that they should declare the causes which impel them to the separation."

3. Use a colon in a formal business letter. 在正式的商業書信中用冒號

- Honorable Senator Warner:

- Dear Ms. Huang:

4. You also use a colon when telling time and between chapter and verse in Bible references. 在表示時間和聖經的章節之間也可以用冒號

- We plan to leave at 1: 00 sharp.

- Psalm 23: 1, "The Lord is my shepherd, I shall not be in want," is a well-known Bible verse.

The semi-colon (;) 分號

You can think of a semi-colon as stronger than a comma but weaker than a period. It has several uses.

你可以把分號想成比逗號強烈，但是比句號弱勢。它有以下幾種用法。

1. It can combine two independent clauses without using a conjunction.
分號可以結合兩個獨立子句而不必使用連接詞

In other words, you can take two short, choppy sentences and link them with a semi-colon as long as they have related ideas.

換句話說，你可以把兩個零散但意義相關的短句用分號連結起來。

- Her mother was from Iran; her father was from Switzerland.

- Tokyo is the capital of Japan; Seoul is the capital of South Korea.

Optional: you can also delete part of the second clause, and replace it with a comma.

另一種寫法：你也可以刪掉第二個子句的其中一些字，並以逗號代替。

- Her mother was from Iran; her father, from Switzerland.

- Tokyo is the capital of Japan; Seoul, of South Korea.

2. You may also use a semi-colon to join independent clauses if they are joined by a word such as *however*, *furthermore*, and *therefore*.
如果兩個獨立子句之間有 however, furthermore, therefore 等字連接時，也可以用分號來合併兩個子句

- Summer in Taiwan is hot; however, it is bearable.

- He did not bring his permission form; therefore, he had to stay home.

3. You can also use the semi-colon to separate items in a series, when there are already commas used. 你也可以使用分號來分隔一連串已經含有逗號的項目

- Her company has offices in three cities: Nashville, Tennessee; Los Angeles, California; and Hong Kong, China.

- We need you to bring red, long-stemmed roses; a vase; and some after-dinner mints.

One reason that I like semi-colons is because they keep sentences flowing. Below is a passage from *Hand Me Another Brick*, a book about leadership, by Chuck Swindoll, and it has several good writing tips. First, see how the author uses bouncing. He is talking about the depression that leaders commonly feel, but rather than write about that abstract fact, he tells a story about his own struggles with discouragement; and he

我愛用分號的理由是因為它可以使句子流暢。以下這段文字來自 Chuck Swindoll 所著的一本有關領導力的書：《Hand Me Another Brick》，裡頭有幾項寫作的訣竅。首先看看作者如何使用「彈跳」技巧，他談到領導者經常會感到意氣消沈，但他不用抽象的比喻，而是描述他自己如何與沮喪情緒奮戰的故事，並引用希爾多·羅斯福的話來支持他的觀點。

includes a quotation from Theodore Roosevelt to make his case. So the author "bounces" between the dry fact and the moving story and quotation. Read Roosevelt's statement carefully. It is so powerful that it is still used 100 years after he wrote it, appearing in both *Hand Me Another Brick* and in a 2007 graduation speech at the school where I teach. If writing is still quoted a hundred years after it was created, it has stood the test of time.

因此該作者是在枯燥事實、感人故事以及引文之間「彈跳」。請仔細閱讀羅斯福的文字,雖然是一百多年前的作品,現在看來仍是鏗鏘有力。《Hand Me Another Brick》這本書以及我在學校 2007 年畢業典禮上都引用了這段話。如果一段文字在經過百年後仍被引用,證明它經得起時間的考驗。

Here is Swindoll's closing passage from his chapter about dealing with discouragement.

以下是 Swindoll 在書中處理沮喪情緒一章的結語。

Many years ago, I became discouraged because of criticism and my optimism eroded as a lengthy chain of events led me into "the pits." Knowing of my need for encouragement, my wife searched for a way to lift my spirits. She found these encouraging comments written by a statesman I have always admired, and used them on a wooden decoupage plaque she gave to me. Consider the words of Theodore Roosevelt:

It is not the critic who counts; not the man who points out how the strong man stumbles, or where the doer of deeds could have done them better. The credit belongs to the man who is actually in the arena, whose face is marred by dust and sweat and blood; who strives valiantly; who errs, and comes short again and again, because there is no effort without error and shortcoming; but who does actually strive to do the deeds; who knows the great enthusiasms, the great devotions; who spends himself in a worthy cause; who at the best knows in the end the triumph of high achievement, and who at the worst, if he fails, at least fails while daring greatly.

Far better it is to dare mighty things, to win glorious triumphs, even though checkered by failure, than to take rank with those poor spirits who neither enjoy much nor suffer much, because they lie in the gray twilight that knows not victory nor defeat.

I repeat the opening statement of this chapter: no leader is exempt from criticism. Don't expect to be. But when it comes, be ready to battle against discouragement, which is poised and ready to strike on the heels of criticism. You can count on it![7]

There are several items I want you to notice. First, see how the author "bounced." Rather than just opening with, "All leaders will be criticized," he tells his own story, including how his wife encouraged him by giving him the plaque with the inspirational quotation. (The author waits until the *last* paragraph to state the fact: "no leader is exempt from criticism.") Second, look how the author closed the first paragraph with a colon to introduce the long quotation. And third, notice how *long* some of the sentences in the quotation are! I do not suggest you write such long sentences, but Teddy Roosevelt knew his English, and his use of semi-colons—seven of them!—keeps the flow going. Also, as former *Roanoke Times* editor Mike Riley once told my students, "If you can use a semi-colon correctly, people will think you're really smart."

以上有幾點值得你注意的地方。第一點是看看作者如何「彈跳」，他不用 All leaders will be criticized 作開頭，而是用自己的故事，以及他太太如何鼓勵他，送給他一塊刻有勵志格言的飾板（作者一直到最後一段才指出事實：no leader is exempt from criticism）。第二點是看作者如何用冒號來作為第一段的結尾，並引介一段長的引文。第三點則是要注意引文中有些句子很長，我並不是建議你要寫很長的句子，但是羅斯福了解自己的英文寫作能力，以及如何使用七個分號來使句子流暢。《Roanoke Times》前任編輯也曾告訴我的學生：「如果你能正確使用分號，別人就會認為你很聰明。」

---

7 Swindoll, Charles. *Hand Me Another Brick: Timeless Lessons in Leadership*, pp. 76-77.

Activity

3.15 Place either a colon (:), semi-colon (;), or comma (,) in the following sentences.

在下列句子中加上冒號 (:)、分號 (;) 或逗號 (,)。

1. All leaders will be criticized however that is no reason to quit.

2. Honorable Mayor Harris

   Please continue to focus on these three areas job creation quality schools and more

   parks.

3. Manila is the capital of the Philippines Hanoi is the capital of Vietnam.

4. Vincent worked hard through the years therefore he graduated with honors.

5. Isabel is excited about her trip to the U.S.! She will visit Honolulu Hawaii Los Angeles

   California and Denver Colorado.

(Answers are in the Answer Key on page 205.)

The dash (—) 破折號

The dash is a useful tool to set off items and keep the flow moving.

破折號可用來分隔項目並保持文字流暢。

1. You can set off ideas in a sentence with dashes. 破折號可把一個句子中的概念分開

You can do the same with commas, but the dash slows down the reader and draws more attention to it.

雖然逗號也有相同作用，但是破折號可以減緩讀者閱讀速度，並吸引其注意力。

- Hong Kong—the Pearl of the Orient—is a fascinating city!

- Algebra class—which is driving me crazy—will be over soon.

- Materialism—the desire for more and more stuff—is a mark of modern life.

2. Like the colon, you can also use a single dash to introduce a person, idea, or surprise. 與冒號一樣，單一的破折號可以引介人物、想法或令人驚訝的事物

- We turned into the parking lot and saw it—the Statue of Liberty!

- Robert searched everywhere and finally found his homework—right in his backpack.

The hyphen (-) 連字號

1. The hyphen may be used with compound adjectives, but it is optional.
連字號可以用在複合形容詞，不過這不是必要的

- After a well-deserved summer break, the students were ready to get back to school.

- After a hard-fought battle, the Allied troops scaled the mountain and continued on to Rome.

- The non-stop flight from Philadelphia to Ireland took less than five hours!

2. Hyphens are also used when writing two-digit numbers or fractions.

連字號也可用在兩位數或分數上

- The White House ordered a twenty-one gun salute to welcome the President of Russia.

- My father is seventy-seven but is still very active.

- Use one-half cup of brown sugar.

▪ **Activity**

3.16 Add a dash (—) or hyphen (-) to these sentences.
在以下句子加上破折號 (—) 或連字號 (-)。

1. Her son is twenty eight but still lives at home.

2. After driving three days, we crested a hill and saw it The Grand Canyon!

3. *The Hurried Child* a book about how we rush our kids to grow up too fast points out a weakness in many families today.

4. Add one quarter cup of milk to that recipe.

(Answers are in the Answer Key on page 206.)

The ellipsis (...) 省略符號

1. Use the ellipsis to show that you have deleted quoted material.
用省略符號表示省略引文的部分內容

- Grace wrote, "I'm having a great time in New Jersey. I'm learning much in my classes...and my roommate is really nice."

2. You can also use this to raise suspense or excitement.
用省略符號來增添懸疑或興奮的氣氛

- Please bring these to class: your book, notebook, a pencil...and a great attitude!

- The elderly lady in the nursing home kept winking at the young male visitor and finally said, "You look just like my third husband...and I've only been married twice!"

3. When writing dialogue, you can show someone hesitating or stuttering.
描寫對話時，可用省略符號來表現遲疑或欲言又止的語氣

- "I just don't know what to do..." Mother worried. "Your father said he would be home by six, and here it is...almost...almost eight o'clock already, and no sign of him," she continued. Mother wrung her hands and her face was twisted with anxiety.

4. The ellipsis also shows that a speaker is continuing, or his voice is trailing off. 省略符號也可表現說話者持續講話或聲音逐漸減弱

(Note: if you <u>end a sentence</u> with an ellipsis, use <u>four</u> dots, not three, because the fourth dot is the period.)

（註：如果你要用省略符號結束一個句子，要用四點而不是三點，因為第四點是句點。）

- "If I ever see you smoking at school again..." Mr. Bowman huffed and shook his finger at Bobby. Frustrated, he sent Bobby back to class as he sank into his chair. "Why does being a principal have to be so hard...?" he thought to himself. "Oh well...just two more years till retirement."

- "Class," Mr. Crawford said. "Since it's snowing, you will be going home early and...."
  The class let out a joyous roar, and no one heard him say they still had homework.

(Parenthesis) 括號

This has several uses, such as marking the acronym for a business or organization.

它有好幾個用法，例如用來註明企業或組織名稱的頭字詞。

• Malaysia belongs to the South East Asian Treaty Organization (SEATO).

But one of my favorite uses for the parenthesis is to act like a whisper, or an aside.

但我最喜歡的括號用法是作為文字的旁白。

• Even though I am an adult, I still keep my childhood habit of always washing my hands before a meal (are you happy, Mom?).
• Our neighbor (God bless her) is the kindest person you'll ever meet.

Italics 斜體字

This font sets off a foreign word, draws attention to something to emphasize, or causes the reader to slow down for a key point.

這種字體是用以表示外國字、或要強調某事物、或讓讀者慢下來注意某要點。

• The French *porc* is a better-sounding word for pork than the German *Scheweinefleisch*.
• Can you *believe* that man? How dare he call *me* a slob.

IN SUM 總結

Use a variety of punctuation to make your language clear and to keep the flow moving. Just do not overuse one particular kind of mark.

使用各式不同的標點符號使你的文字清楚流暢，但不要過度使用某一特定的標點符號。

■ Activity

3.17 Add punctuation to make each sentence clearer or stronger. There may be more than one option for each.

為下列句子加上標點符號使它們更清楚有力，每個句子可能會用到一個以上的標點符號。

1. Here we go again you have lost your keys for the third time this week.

2. It rained however we still had a good time.

3. She looked stunning in her new solid blue dress.

4. Elma that sweet lady was so generous to give each child a quarter.

5. Please bring the following hi liters, colored pencils, and a dozen donuts.

6. The Bible begins at Genesis 1 1.

7. He has a lazy streak nevertheless he still passed with a D.

8. Aunt Maggie my favorite aunt always prepared a Thanksgiving feast!

9. The Potomac River flows west to east the Shenandoah River flows south to north.

10. After a long day on curvy roads, we finally got there Hualien.

(Answers are in the Answer Key on page 206.)

STEP 9 — Vary Sentence Lengths & Patterns
變化句長和句型

If you have ever ridden a train, do you often feel like falling asleep soon after taking a seat? One reason may be the rhythm. The repetition puts us to sleep. The same is true of writing. If you repeat the same sentence lengths and patterns, you will bore your audience. Mix it up; do not be afraid of long sentences, but do not overuse them either.

如果你搭過火車，你是否一坐上車很快就想睡覺呢？原因就在於火車的節奏感。重複的東西讓我們想睡，寫作也是一樣。如果你重複相同的句長和句型，會讓讀者感到乏味。所以要有變化，不要怕使用長句，但也不要過度使用。

I like this gem from *The Art of Readable Writing*:

我喜歡這則從《The Art of Readable Writing》書上節錄的佳例：

> Whenever you can shorten a sentence, do.
> And one always can.
> The best sentence?
> The shortest.
> —Gustav Flaubert

Take this example:

再看以下的例子：

> Hsinchu is a city. It is a city in Taiwan. It is located in northwest Taiwan. Hsinchu is about an hour south of Taipei. The name "Hsinchu" means "New Bamboo" in Chinese. Hsinchu is an important city in Taiwan. It is important because it is the capital of Taiwan's computer industry. Hsinchu is home to two famous universities. They are called Tsing Hua University and Chiao Tung University. Hsinchu is home to the Science Park as well.

Boring, right? The grammar, spelling, and facts are correct, but the sentence structure is dull and cluttered.

很無聊，不是嗎？它的文法、拼字和資訊都是正確的，但是句子結構太單調而且鬆散。

■ Activity

3.18 Now, rewrite it, varying the sentence length and patterns.

現在改寫以上的例子，變化它的句子長度和句型。

_____

_____

_____

_____

_____

(Suggested answers are in the Answer Key on page 207.)

Break up long sentences 長句切成短句

One of the best ways to make your writing clearer is to break up long, confusing sentences. I once edited a paper with *one sentence containing 73 words*! Look at this 45-word tangle:

要使文意清楚的一個好方法，就是把易混淆的長句切成短句。我還曾經修改過一個長達 73 字的長句呢！先看看以下這 45 個字糾纏不清的句子：

- This research successfully develops a set of software and hardware module components for the joint servo and distributed robot control system which includes the humanoid robot mechanism, the joint servo actuator, the robot central controller, the ZigBee wireless network, and the host graphic user interface.

One sentence—confusing! Here it is, rewritten:

只用一個句子，令人費解！改寫之後如下：

- This research successfully develops a set of software and hardware module components for the joint servo and distributed robot control system. This system includes the humanoid robot mechanism, the joint servo actuator, the robot central controller, the ZigBee wireless network, and the host graphic user interface.

Two sentences—much better!

兩個句子就好多了！

Dialogue 對話

In addition, to vary sentence patterns, skilled writers use these twin tricks often: <u>dialogue</u> and so-called "<u>thought shots</u>." They let the reader know what a character is thinking, and can move action along quickly. Plus, they make one's writing more natural and smooth.

此外，句型要有變化，熟練的作者經常會使用兩種技巧：對話和所謂的「內心思索」。這兩種技巧可以讓讀者了解文中人物的想法，讓劇情迅速展開。另外，也可以使作品更加自然和順暢。

Dialogue is simply engaging two or more people in conversation. Have a look:

對話就是讓兩人或多人進行交談，例如：

- Larry wondered if Dad could help him fix his van's air conditioner.
  Dialogue: "Dad," Larry asked, "Could you check the freon in my van?"
- Carol told the other children about her trip to China.
  Dialogue: "My favorite thing in China was the zoo," Carol explained. "I saw dolphins and sharks, and even got to touch a starfish."

Here is another example from *Hand Me Another Brick*. This time, the author uses dialogue to discuss how new ideas usually spark opposition. What effect does the dialogue have? Note also how the author uses a variety of punctuation and sentence lengths. Some sentences have only one or two words!

以下是《Hand Me Another Brick》書中的另一個例子，這次作者使用對話來討論為何新的想法往往會招致反對。對話在此會有何種效果？注意作者如何使用各種不同的標點符號以及句子長度。有些句子甚至只有一兩個字。

> New ideas seem to go through three channels. First, rejection. You have an idea for something new. The person you tell it to says, "It won't work." You ask, "Why?" He replies, "Because we've tried it before." Or, "No one's ever done that before." It's rejected. The second channel is toleration: "Well, I'll allow it, as long as...." The third channel, the ideal response, is acceptance: "Let's go!"[8]

I think the use of dialogue improves the passage, because it makes the ideas understandable by using responses we have all heard before.

我認為使用對話有助於此篇文字的效果，這種我們經常聽到的對話回應使文中的概念更容易理解。

Caution: Do not overuse dialogue; too much can make your writing sluggish. Just sprinkle it in here and there, when appropriate.

小心：切勿過度使用對話，太多的對話會使文氣阻滯，只有在適當時機才偶一為之。

---

8 Swindoll, Charles. *Hand Me Another Brick: Timeless Lessons in Leadership*, p. 12.

Thought shots, in contrast, are simply writing what a character is thinking, and since you are the author, you can make the character think whatever you want! Feel the power!

相對地,「內心思索」只是描寫人物心中的想法。既然你是作者,你可以讓文中的人物如你所願的思考,好好感受一下身為作者的力量吧!

- Alice did not want to look foolish.

  Thought shot: "Don't be a fool," Alice thought.

- Beatrice did not want to see Charles again, but had to fake it.

  Thought shot: "Oh no, I can't believe Charles is here," Beatrice gasped to herself, but quickly regained composure and put on a smile: "Why Charles," she said, "how nice to see you again."

- The students thoroughly enjoyed the writing class.

  Thought shot: "What a super writing class!" the students thought to themselves. "I cannot think of any place I would rather be, absorbing all this precious knowledge!"

This use of a thought shot is a big advantage of books over movies. Books can more easily reveal what characters are thinking.

在書籍中使用內心思索比在電影中的效果更好,因為寫作更能精細描繪人物的思考。

IN SUM 總結

Avoid the "Railroad Syndrome." Mix up your sentence lengths and patterns. Use some dialogue or thought shots, when appropriate, to make your writing more realistic and help your readers identify with the characters.

避免「火車症候群」,讓你的句長和句型充滿變化。在適當的地方使用一些對話或內心思索,使文章更加寫實,並讓讀者認同文中的人物。

Activity

3.19 Take these sentences and try to rewrite them as either dialogues or thought shots.

將下列句子改為對話或內心思索的句子。

1. Mrs. Chen gave the children a map of Mainland China.

_____

2. Anna and her mother argued over Anna's use of the computer.

_____

3. Hannah could not decide whether to sign up for Spanish or French.

_____

(Suggested answers are in the Answer Key on page 207.)

STEP 10 Use Active Voice
使用主動語態

With active voice, the subject is doing the action. With passive voice, however, the action is being done to the subject and the sentence's meaning is delayed until the end.

主動語態中由主詞執行動作，而被動語態中的主詞是承受動作，句意要到最後才會清楚。

In most cases, write in active voice. You often find passive voice in government documents or in cases where someone may be trying to avoid responsibility! I once saw this sign on a school door:

大多數情況下應使用主動語態，在政府文件或某些想要逃避責任的情況下才會看到被動語態。我有一次就在學校大門看到以下的告示：

> • Students entering without a pass will be punished.

This is passive voice, and it leaves several questions opened. Who will punish me? How will I be punished? The same idea, in active voice, would be:

這是個被動語態，因此顯得不夠清楚。究竟是誰要來處罰我？如何處罰？如果使用主動語態就會變成：

> • The Administration will punish any student who enters without a pass.

PASSIVE 被動		**ACTIVE** 主動
• The tail **was wagged** by Lucky.	→	Lucky wagged his tail.
• The photos **were loaded** onto the PC by Harmony.	→	Harmony loaded her photos onto the PC.
• The answer **was written** on the board by Jonas.	→	Jonas wrote the answer on the board.

Hint: Passive voice is usually longer, sounds awkward, often uses the word "by," and is unclear as to who is doing what!

提示：被動語態句子通常較長、語氣不順、常需用到 by、而且不清楚是誰在做什麼事。

IN SUM 總結

In sum: Generally speaking, use active voice.

總結：一般而言，多使用主動語態。

The difference between a successful person and others is not a lack of strength,
not a lack of knowledge, but rather in a lack of will.

成功人士與他人的區別不在力量和知識，而是意志力。

—Vince Lombardi

■ Activity

3.20 Write "A" for active or "P" for passive, for each sentence.

在主動語態的句子前寫 A，被動語態句子前寫 P。

1. _____ Andrew vacuumed the floor.

2. _____ The thank you note was written by Jimmy.

3. _____ Interstate 81 was built by the highway department.

4. _____ Michael lifted weights during the summer to bulk up.

5. _____ The letters were delivered by the mailman.

6. _____ Mrs. Brown taught the grammar points and the students understood the information.

7. _____ Passive voice was taught by Mr. Dreyer.

8. _____ Passive voice is generally to be avoided in writing.

9. _____ Use active voice when writing.

10. _____ I hope you are improving your English skills!

(Answers are in the Answer Key on page 208.)

3.21 Now, take these passive sentences and make them active.

把以下的被動語態句子改為主動語態。

1. The book was snatched by the lad.

_____

2. The call was answered by Diane.

_____

3. Two tents were pitched by the Boy Scouts.

_____

4. Tears were shed by Mrs. Longthorne.

_____

5. The postman has been bitten by several dogs.

_____

6. A love of history and geography was given to me by my brother Mark.

_____

(Suggested answers are in the Answer Key on page 208.)

11 End with a Bang
動人的結語

You are almost done!

就快大功告成了！

As you wrap up your masterpiece, be sure to end with a *bang,* (and not a whimper).

在你完成大作之際，記得要有個動人的結語（不要無力呻吟）。

Imagine a paper where Charlene has been writing about a time from her youth.

想像 Charlene 寫了一篇描述她年輕歲月的文字。

My parents forbade me to go out, but I sneaked out the window late one night, slid silently through the dark, and hopped into my boyfriend's car. "They'll never know," I smugly said to myself.

After a night on the town, I silently slipped home, gingerly put the key in the lock, padded into the kitchen...to see mother sitting up, hands on her hips, waiting for me!

Now, it is time for Charlene to end her story. What is the better closing?

現在 Charlene 要結束這篇文章，以下哪一個結語比較好？

> A. "Mom grounded me for two weeks, and I learned so much from that important lesson."
>
> B. "Two weeks."

I prefer ending "B," because it is so short.

我喜歡 B，因為它很簡短。

Imagine concluding an essay about the need for better farming technology to feed the hungry world:

再想像有篇文章呼籲創新農業技術來援助全球的飢荒，要如何作結語呢？

> With some 800 million hungry people in the world, it is essential to find better ways to grow food. Otherwise, millions will go hungry, and many conflicts may break out when countries cannot feed their teeming populations, and these conflicts could easily lead to wars.

How is that for an ending? For one thing, it ends on a negative note, "starvation, conflicts, and wars." But the ending also leaves us hanging. Instead, maybe add this sentence to the end.

以上的結語如何？營造了 starvation, conflicts, wars 的情境，使得語氣太負面了。而且這樣的結語讓我們覺得語氣還沒結束，不如再加上以下這個句子。

- Working hand in hand, however, surely the scientists and nations of the world can find ways to boost food production while also protecting the environment.

See the difference? This ends on a more positive note and sums up the author's point.

可以看出差異嗎？這個結語就比較正面，而且可以總結作者的重點。

In my years of teaching, I find many writers struggle with endings. Perhaps the writer has run out of things to say, or is just tired. Whatever the reason, many conclusions leave the reader "hanging." Create a powerful ending that restates your thesis, the point you have tried to prove. Do you want your reader to do something? Believe something? Buy something? Seal the deal. Review Step 1, about finding a good hook, because some of the same ideas also apply to good endings. You may use a quotation, questions, story, or joke to wrap up your piece.

以我多年教學的經驗，我發現很多人都覺得結語很困難。也許他們已經把該說的都說完了，或者只是覺得累了。不論什麼原因，很多人寫的結論都讓讀者覺得言不盡意。文章應該要有動人的結尾，用以重述你的主旨或你想證明的要點。例如你想要讀者去做某事？相信某事？購買某物品？一定要明確作總結。現在回顧步驟一看看如何設定好的切入點，其中有些寫法也可以應用在結語，例如使用引言、問題、故事或笑話等來完成你的作品。

IN SUM 總結

End on a strong note: an ironic twist, a call to action, an appeal. End
with a bang, not a whimper.

以有力的方式結束——如諷刺性的轉折、呼籲採取行動、請求。以動人的方式結語，不要虛弱的
低吟。

Opportunity: Nowhere, or Now Here.
The Choice is Yours.

機會存在與否，都是由你決定。

–Zig Ziglar

STEP 12 Finish with Formatting
完稿前檢查格式

As you wrap up your work, here are a few final points.

Format properly. Ask your teacher for any specific requirements, but generally this is standard:

- Typed, double-spaced
- 1" margins all around
- Justified margins, so the right side of your text is in a straight line, not jagged
- Size 11-12 font
- Clear font: Times New Roman or Arial are common; avoid odd or unclear fonts
- Put your name, the date, and the teacher's name on it, usually in the top-right corner.
- Number the papers of the document

Reread carefully. If you typed your essay, print a copy; most folks can proofread better on paper than on a computer screen. If possible, ask someone to read your work, and you can read his or hers. Make editing marks on the paper; you will probably find items to delete, move, or add. Make sure the ideas flow logically. Read it aloud to yourself. Most of what we write makes *perfect* sense to *us*; after all, we wrote it! But when you read it aloud, or ask someone else to read this, you may see that some things do need revision.

完成寫作前，最後還有幾件事情要注意：

要有適當的格式，問問你的老師是否有特定的格式要求，以下是一般的標準：

- 打字、雙行行距
- 版面邊界各留一吋
- 文章邊緣一致，所以右邊要對齊，不要參差不齊
- 字型大小爲 11-12 號
- 字體清晰：通常使用 Times New Roman 或 Arial，避免使用古怪或不清楚的字體
- 寫下你的姓名、日期和教師姓名，通常置於右上方
- 文章要標示頁數

把文章仔細重讀一遍，如果你是用電腦打字，就列印出來閱讀。大多數人覺得在紙張上校對比在電腦螢幕上容易。如果可能的話，請別人來讀你的文章，而你可以讀他們的文章。在文章上註記修訂的符號，例如要刪除、移動或增修其中的文字。要確定文意的發展符合邏輯，可以大聲朗讀出來聽聽看。我們看自己寫的文字通常都覺得很合理，畢竟那是自己的作品。但是當你大聲唸出來或請別人幫你看時，可能就會發現需要修改的地方。

Common Proofreading/Editing Marks 常用的修訂符號		
Mark	**Meaning**	**Example**
⌃	insert （插入）	We will to find the store. try
℘	delete （刪除）	Try to rememmber to spell words correctly.
#	insert space （插入空格）	Summervacation is a good break. #
‿	remove a space （移走空格）	We went to the fire house.
≡	capitalize （大寫）	Have you ever visited hsinchu?
SP	spelling （拼字）	Rite this down on your paper. SP
⌄⌄	wrong word （用字錯誤）	It is two cold to go swimming. WW
⌐_	switch word order （調換字序）	We visited Paul Uncle.
⊄	make a new paragraph （另起新的一段）	This year, however, will be different.

And remember, as we discussed earlier, <u>writing is a process of continual revision</u>. Thomas Jefferson's Declaration of Independence had marks and revisions all over it! Jefferson could have become arrogant, had his feelings hurt, and walked out. But he stayed. He was patient, did not take the criticism personally, and after days of deliberations, was awarded approval of the final version. Mr. Jefferson's masterpiece later became world

記住我們之前提過的：寫作是一個持續修訂的過程。湯瑪斯・傑佛遜的〈獨立宣言〉被寫上各種註記和修訂符號，他如果表現傲慢或覺得自尊受損，大可拂袖而去。但是他留下來耐心以對，不把別人的批評當作人身攻擊。經過幾天的深思審議後，終於確認最後的版本。傑佛遜先生的傑作之後也廣為世人所流傳。這個故事的重點在於，如果傑佛遜的

famous. The point? If Jefferson's work was criticized, picked apart, and revised, then surely you and I can take a little constructive criticism from people who care about us and our writing. A deal?

作品都會被批評、吹毛求疵和修訂，那你和我當然也可從關心我們文章的人那邊接受一些建設性的批評。你同意嗎？

When you have completed Step 12, turn in your paper, whether it is to your teacher, an editor, or the newspaper, and be pleased knowing that you did your best!

當你完成這12個步驟，也就是你交出作品的時候，不論是交給你的老師、編輯或是報社，你都要為自己的全力以赴而感到欣喜！

IN SUM 總結

Make your finished product look neat and professional. If it looks like you took your work seriously, others are more likely to take it—and you—seriously too.

你最終完成的作品應該看起來整齊專業。如果你的文章看起來是經過努力的成果，別人對你的文章和對你個人也會加以尊重。

Answer Key
解答

ANSWER KEY 解答

This answer key follows the exercises in Part B & Part C. Again, writing is not like math, so these are not the only "right" answers. These answers are here to give you some guidance to your writing and let you know if you are on the right track or not. Especially when it comes to things like choosing a title, you have much freedom. Be creative.

以下是 Part B 及 Part C 的練習題的解答。再一次提醒，寫作可不是數學，所以這些並不是唯一的「正確」答案，它們只是給你寫作上的一些指引，讓你知道你是否朝較好的方向前進。尤其像在選擇寫作題目這種練習題上，你就有很大的空間，記得要發揮你的創意。

Part B

Activity 2.1 (p. 78)

1. depressing
2. boring
3. bored
4. amazing
5. embarrassing

6. disgusting
7. confusing
8. depressed
9. embarrassed
10. interested

Activity 2.2 (p. 84)

1. swimming
2. taking; swimming
3. get; go

4. get
5. driving

Activity 2.3 (p. 88)

1. safely; adverb
2. quiet; noun
3. quietly; adverb

4. anger; verb
5. gentle; adjective
6. gently; adverb

7. anger; noun

8. happiness; noun

9. angrily; adverb

10. nervous; adjective

Activity 2.4 (p. 89)

(Answer will vary.)

1. Megan skipped <u>happily</u> home, because school was over for the year.

2. Dan <u>angrily</u> slammed the phone down, after his girlfriend hung up on him.

3. "Don't be <u>nervous</u>," Mom said. "You'll do fine on your test today."

4. Richard was driving <u>dangerously</u>, so the police pulled him over.

5. Many people feel <u>sad</u> in the winter, because of the cloudy weather and short days.

Activity 2.5 (p. 92)

1. Has this ever happened to you?/

   Have you ever experienced this before?/

   Have you ever felt this way before?

2. Have you ever had it before?/

   Have you ever experienced it before?

3. Culture shock is common./

   It is normal to have culture shock when you travel./

   Culture shock is a normal occurrence when you go someplace new.

Activity 2.6 (p. 100)

1. the

2. ---

3. the

4. ---

5. ---

6. The

7. The; the

8. ---

9. the; the

11. ---

10. ---; the

12. the

Activity 2.7 (p. 102)

1. Take it easy and go for a walk./Relax for a while and go for a walk.

2. I know you are upset that your girlfriend dumped you, but try to take it easy. You'll find somebody else./
I know you are upset that your girlfriend dumped you, but try to keep perspective. You'll find somebody else./
I know you are upset that your girlfriend dumped you, but try to not let it get to you. You'll find somebody else.

3. Studying for test is hard, but it is important to relax some./
Studying for test is hard, but it is important to get away from it some.

Activity 2.8 (p. 104)

1. Your smile will draw people to you./Smiling will draw people to you.

2. Everyone liked Annie because of her smile./
Everyone liked Annie because of her bright smile./
Everyone liked Annie because of her cheerful smile.

3. Smile while you are giving a speech, and your audience will probably like you more./
Have a smile while you are giving a speech, and your audience will probably like you more.

Activity 2.9 (p. 107)

1. ✗ → The Chinese <u>are</u> known for their good work ethic.

2. ✗ → Education <u>is</u> valued in most Chinese families.

3. ✔

4. ✗ → Watching fish swim in an aquarium <u>has</u> been proven to reduce blood pressure.

   (Careful: the subject is "watching," not "fish," so you need a *singular* verb: has.)

5. ✗ → Seafood <u>is</u> a big part of the Japanese diet.

6. ✔

7. ✗ → The United States <u>is</u> a big country.

   (Little-known historical note: in the early days of the US, it was referred to as a plural noun, "the United States are," but since the American Civil War of the 1860s it has been used as a *singular* noun.)

8. ✔

9. ✗ → The ducks <u>are</u> swimming gracefully.

10. ✗ → "Children <u>are</u> a blessing from the Lord," the Bible <u>says</u>.

Activity 2.10 (p. 109)

1. <u>Learning</u> English takes time.

2. <u>Reading</u> is good for your mind.

3. <u>Watching</u> TV can be a waste of time.

4. <u>Having</u> a pet can keep older people healthy.

Part C

Activity 3.1 (p. 118)

1. Topic:

   Do not worry/Face the Future with Confidence/Look on the Bright Side

2. Topic:

   The Importance of Family/The Link between Family and Country

3. Topic:

   Study History/The Importance of History/Know Your Past to Plan Your Future

4. Topic:

Life is Uncertain/Work Hard and Pray Hard/Plan for the Future

5. Topic:

Persistence/Never Give Up/Patience Makes You Stronger

6. Topic:

Go for It!/Seize the Moment!/Grab Life before it Grabs You

Activity 3.2 (p. 122)

These are some possible titles to replace the original, boring ones.

以下是一些示範的題目寫法，用以取代原有無趣的題目。

1. The Invention that Changed the World/We Have Been Talking Ever Since!

2. The Car King/Where Would We Be Without Ford?/Without Ford, We Would Be Walking.

3. The Day that Will Live in Infamy/The Sleeping Giant Awakes/Attack from the Air

4. Gymnastics Is My Life/Read or Die/Video Gaming and Me

Again, these are just a few suggestions. When it comes to titles, the options are limitless. Just be sure the title is unique, clear, and grabs the reader.

再次提醒，這只是一些建議。題目的可能性是無限的，只要是獨特、清楚而能吸引讀者注意，就是好題目。

Activity 3.3 (p. 132)

Here are a few possibilities you could easily use.

以下是幾個你可隨時使用的答案。

1. crash/explosion/boom

2. feast/banquet

3. hobo/panhandler/beggar

4. chandelier

Activity 3.4 (p. 132)

These are just some suggested sentences. Your answers will be different.

以下只是建議的句子，你的寫法可以不一樣。

1.

Dull:

I ordered a large hamburger at Burger King.

Better:

I ordered a Whopper® at Burger King.

2.

Dull:

Charlie Brown always liked the girl with red hair.

Better:

Charlie Brown always liked the redhead.

3.

Dull:

Bryce wore formal business clothes to the interview.

Better:

Bryce wore a suit to the interview.

Activity 3.5 (p. 139)

1. zoomed/sped/flew/careened/crept/inched

   (Note how the verb controls the speed: the first four verbs imply a fast speed while the last two imply slowness.)

2. gobbled/inhaled/wolfed down/gulped down/picked at/nibbled

   (Again, the verb sets the speed: the first four verbs say Victor ate quickly while the last two imply he was not hungry and ate slowly.)

3. chatted/conversed/reminisced

4. bolted/sped/dashed/careened/wobbled/doddered/stumbled/staggered

(Here too the verb sets the speed: in the first four, the toddler moved quickly, with more control, while the last four verbs imply slowness and unsteadiness.)

Activity 3.6 (p. 139)

Sample answers. Yours will be different.

以下只是解答範例，你可以有不同的寫法。

1.

Dull:

Mr. Han drank two beers.

Better:

Mr. Han guzzled/put down/gulped down two beers.

2.

Dull:

The bird flew from branch to branch.

Better:

The bird darted/zipped/flitted/zoomed from branch to branch.

3.

Dull:

The police officers looked at the crime reports.

Better:

The police officers pored over/combed through/sweated over/bore through the crime reports.

(Note how these verbs imply hard work: the officers were intensely examining the evidence.)

Activity 3.7 (p. 143)

1. We regret to inform you that we are unable to provide assistance at this present moment. (25 syllables)

→ Sorry, but we cannot help you now. (9 syllables)

2. The hot atmospheric conditions were oppressive. (13 syllables)

   → The heat was awful. (5 syllables)

Activity 3.8 (p. 149)

1. If I had one free week and an extra NT$30,000, I would pack my swimsuit, sunscreen, and towel and take my family to Kenting! I love Kenting. Its scenery of azure sea and jagged mountains rivals Hawaii. Kenting's beaches are especially welcoming in the winter, when North Taiwan is cold and rainy. Yet the island's southern tip is warm enough to allow swimming. But there is much to do out of the water too. You can rent a scooter and explore the beautiful Hengchun Peninsula. For the more energetic, you can hike *Dajianshan* inside the National Park for a commanding panorama of the area. End your days with a seafood dinner or savor a Southeast Asian meal at Tricycle restaurant in downtown Hengchun. Enjoy Kenting!

2. There are many qualities one looks for in a friend, but three stand out. For me, honesty is essential. If you cannot expect the truth from a friend, whom else can you trust? Second, loyalty is important. A faithful friend will stick with you through good times and bad. Third, encouragement is a key trait. We live in a negative world, so an encouraging friend will bring out the best in you. Friends are important, because we eventually resemble the people we spend time with.

Activity 3.9 (p. 153)

1. yet

2. First

3. However

4. Second

5. and

6. under

7. Third

8. during

9. When

10. Lastly

Activity 3.10 (p. 160)

1. "Turn it down," Mom asked.

2. Please remain seated.

3. "Stop it, David!" Harmony snapped./
   "Stop it, David!" Harmony barked./
   "Stop it, David!" Harmony shouted.

Activity 3.11 (p. 160)

Sample answers. Yours will be different.

以下只是解答範例，你可以有不同的寫法。

1.

Cluttered:

You are highly encouraged to attend the meeting.

Uncluttered:

You need to attend the meeting.

2.

Cluttered:

After a careful review of your petition, it has been determined that your request for a salary adjustment cannot be granted at this time, and for this we deeply express our regret.

Uncluttered:

Sorry, but we cannot give you a raise right now.

3.

Cluttered:

Raising children involves a major commitment of time, love, and emotional and physical energy.

Uncluttered:

Raising children is a huge job.

Activity 3.12 (p. 163)

1. <u>Learning</u> a foreign language is about as difficult as <u>learning</u> to play a musical instrument.

2. Learning a foreign language requires <u>work</u>, <u>dedication</u>, and <u>self-discipline</u>.

3. Three reasons why Kenting is such a popular resort are the <u>beautiful scenery</u>, the <u>warm climate</u>, and the <u>fun outdoor activities</u>.

Activity 3.13 (p. 166)

1. Its strong winds give Hsinchu its nickname: The Windy City.

2. After years of planning and hard work, it had arrived: graduation day!

3. Please bring these items to the picnic: paper plates, cups, ice, and sandwiches.

Activity 3.14 (p. 166)

Your answers will vary, but here are some examples.

以下只是解答範例，你可以有不同的寫法。

1. After eleven hours on the plane, we had arrived: California!

2. Please pack these things for the trip: your passport, a camera, and lots of money!

3. "I am pleased to announce the winner of the geography contest: Megan Wu!"

Activity 3.15 (p. 171)

1. All leaders will be criticized; however, that is no reason to quit.

2. Honorable Mayor Harris:
   Please continue to focus on these three areas: job creation, quality schools, and more parks.
   (Note: the comma after "schools" is optional.)

3. Manila is the capital of the Philippines; Hanoi is the capital of Vietnam.

4. Vincent worked hard through the years; therefore, he graduated with honors.

5. Isabel is excited about her trip to the U.S.! She will visit Honolulu, Hawaii; Los Angeles, California; and Denver, Colorado.

Activity 3.16 (p. 174)

1. Her son is twenty-eight but still lives at home.

2. After driving three days, we crested a hill and saw it—The Grand Canyon!

3. *The Hurried Child*—a book about how we rush our kids to grow up too fast—points out a weakness in many families today.

4. Add one-quarter cup of milk to that recipe.

Activity 3.17 (p. 177)

1. Here we go again: you have lost your keys for the third time this week.
   (Or you can also use a dash or ellipsis.)

2. It rained; however, we still had a good time.

3. She looked stunning in her new, solid-blue dress.

4. Elma—that sweet lady—was so generous to give each child a quarter.
   (Or you can use commas to speed up the sentence or even ellipsis to slow it down even more, for emphasis.)

5. Please bring the following: hi-liters, colored pencils, and a dozen donuts.

6. The Bible begins at Genesis 1:1.

7. He has a lazy streak; nevertheless, he still passed with a D.

8. Aunt Maggie—my favorite aunt—always prepared a Thanksgiving feast!
   (This is like sentence 4: you may use dashes, commas, or ellipsis.)

9. The Potomac River flows west to east; the Shenandoah River flows south to north.

10. After a long day on curvy roads, we finally got there: Hualien.

Activity 3.18 (p. 179)

Hsinchu, about an hour south of Taipei, is a city in Northwest Taiwan. Hsinchu, whose name means "New Bamboo" in Chinese, is an important city for several reasons. It is the capital of Taiwan's computer industry, as well as the home of the famous Tsing Hua University, Chiao Tung University, and the Science Park. (Three sentences)

Activity 3.19 (p. 183)

Because there is such an array of choices you could make, you will find two possible answers for each, as samples.

因為寫作的可能性太多了，以下每題都提供兩種可能的答案。

1.

A. "Look kids," Mrs. Chen said. "I have a map of Mainland China for each of you!"

"Hooray!" the kids all shouted in unison.

B. "Children, we brought you all a little treat from our trip to China," Mrs. Chen told the expectant children. "A map of China...one for each of you!"

"Thanks, Mrs. Chen!" the children squealed excitedly.

2.

A. "Mom, I need the computer now," Anna said, with a rising edge to her voice.

"You've been online for two hours already," Mom snapped back. "Off!"

"But if I don't download those notes for history tonight, I might get a D, and would *that* make you happy?" Anna blurted out with a red face.

"OK, you win. Download the stupid notes," Mom muttered as she stomped away. "Why does raising teenagers have to be so hard?" she thought to herself.

B. "Anna, time for supper. Turn off the computer and come to the table."

"OK Mom, as soon as I finish this last email."

"No, I mean *now*," her mother ordered sharply.

"Why do you have to be so bossy?" Anna screamed!

3.

A. "Hmm, what should I take next year?" Hannah wondered. "I've always wanted to go to Paris, but Spanish might help me more if I ever went to South America or Mexico."

B. "Spanish or French? Spanish or French?" Hannah pondered over and over. "Most of my friends are going to take Spanish, but John is going to take French, and he sure is good-looking!"

Activity 3.20 (p. 186)

1. A	6. A
2. P	7. P
3. P	8. P
4. A	9. A
5. P	10. A

Activity 3.21 (p. 187)

1. The lad snatched the book.

2. Diane answered the call.

3. The Boy Scouts pitched two tents.

4. Mrs. Longthorne shed tears.

5. Several dogs have bitten the postman.

6. My brother Mark gave me a love of history and geography.

Appendix
附錄

1 Words Often Confused
容易混淆的字詞

Since English has the world's largest vocabulary, it is normal that many words would look or sound similar. These words confuse native speakers also. I once saw this sign at a car wash:

因為英文是全世界詞彙量最多的語言，也難怪很多字詞看起來或聽起來很類似。這些字詞連以英語為母語的人士都很容易混淆。我有次在洗車場看到這個標示：

- NOW EXCEPTING CREDIT CARDS[1]

A friend once saw this in a high school classroom:

我的朋友在一間高中教室內還看到：

- Everybody past there exams.[2]

Can you find the three errors in the two sentences above?

你能找出上述兩個句子中的三個錯誤嗎？

Below is a partial list of tricky words. Also, many of these have several meanings; I am just including the more common ones. Watch out for these words often confused:

以下列出某些容易混淆的字，其中很多字有幾個不同的意義，我只列出其最普遍的意義。要仔細分辨這些常令人混淆不清的字：

| accept
or
except? | **accept** (v.) to agree to or receive 接受
• I can accept your agreement; let's sign the contract. |
| | **except** (prep.) with the exception of 除⋯之外
• We are open daily except for Sundays. |

---

1 NOW <u>ACCEPTING</u> CREDIT CARDS
2 Everybody <u>passed</u> <u>their</u> exams.

advice or **advise?**	**advice** (n.) counsel or guidance 忠告 • Can you please give me some advice? **advise** (v.) to give advice, warning, or recommendation 建議 • I would advise you to stay home and study tonight; you have a test tomorrow!
affect or **effect?**	**affect** (v.) to produce an effect upon or influence someone or something 影響 • Smoking and drinking can affect your health. **effect** (n.) something that follows a cause 效果，效應 • Many believe pollution causes the Greenhouse Effect.
alot or **a lot** or **allot?**	**alot** This is not a word! Never use it. **a lot** (adv.) much, or often (However, this is informal language, so generally do not write it.) 多 • Our new car is a lot nicer than the old one. **allot** (v.) to assign or distribute 分配 • We will allot the hotel rooms based on who checks in first.
altar or **alter?**	**altar** (n.) a high place used in worship 聖壇 • The bride and groom lit the candle on the altar during the wedding. **alter** (v.) to change or adjust 改變 • When we alter our attitudes, we can alter the direction of our lives!
among or **between?**	**among** (prep.) in the middle of or surrounded by; usually used when referring to two or more people or items 在…之中 • I feel comfortable when I am among my friends. **between** (prep.) in the middle of (This is the preferred word when there are two items, but this is not an absolute rule.) 在…之間 • Joann sat between her mom and dad.

breath or **breathe?**	**breath** (n.) air expelled from the lungs 氣息 • Do you have any gum? I have bad breath today. **breathe** (v.) to inhale and exhale 呼吸 • "Breathe deeply," the doctor told her patient.
capital or **capitol?**	**capital** (n.) the capital city of a state or nation 首都 • Berlin is the capital of Germany. (n.) money used to invest in business 資本 • The businesswoman needed more capital to open her florist shop. **capitol** (n.) the primary government building of a state or nation 美國國會或州議會大廈 • The capitol in Washington D.C. is where the U.S. Congress meets. (Hint: The capitol in Washington has a round dome, which reminds me of the letter "o" in the word "capitol.")
conscience or **conscious** or **conscientious?**	**conscience** (n.) a sense of knowing right and wrong 良知 • If your conscience tells you not to do something, you should probably not do it. **conscious** (adj.) capable of thought; being awake and alert 有意識的 • He was conscious even though he had a major heart attack. **conscientious** (adj.) following your conscience; upright; careful 誠實的；勤勉的 • The boss always praised her conscientious employee for working hard.
definitely or **defiantly?**	**definitely** (adv.) without question or doubt 一定 • He told me he will definitely pay me the money tomorrow. **defiantly** (adv.) acting with rebellion and disobedience 挑戰地 • The two-year-old defiantly kept crawling out of his bed.

dessert or **desert?**	**dessert** (n.) the sweet dish served after a meal 點心 • "Would you like apple or pumpkin pie for dessert?" Grandma asked.
	desert (n.) an area with little rainfall 沙漠 • China's Gobi Desert is huge. (v.) to quit or flee from a duty 遺棄 • The soldiers were caught after they tried to desert from the army. (Hint: when used as a verb, this word is pronounced like the sweet after-dinner dish!)
descent or **dissent?**	**descent** (n.) birth or lineage 後代 • Many people in the U.S. are of German or English descent. (n.) the act of going down 下降 • "Our plane is now in its descent to the airport," the pilot said.
	dissent (n.; v.) a difference of opinion; to have a difference of opinion or belief 不同意 • Dictatorships try to crush all dissent, while democracies tolerate and even welcome it.
ensure or **insure?**	**ensure** (v.) to make sure or guarantee 保證 • Can you ensure that our hotel room will look as good as it does in the Internet pictures?
	insure (v.) to buy insurance 投保 • Always insure your car before you drive it.
fewer or **less?**	**fewer** (adj.) less, but used with <u>countable</u> nouns 較少的 • We have fewer people this week than last week.
	less (adj.) of a limited number, but usually used with <u>non-countable</u> nouns 較少的 • Chicken has less fat than pork.

its or **it's?**	**its** (pron.; adj.) showing possession or relating to itself 它的 • The puppy kept chasing its tail.
	it's (contraction) it is or it has 它是；它有 • It's going to rain, so bring your umbrella.

loose or **lose** or **lost** or **loss?**	**loose** (adj.) not tight 寬鬆的 • Since I went on a diet, all my clothes feel loose.
	lose (v.) to not win 輸 • Nobody likes to lose a game, but that is a part of life.
	lost (adj.) unable to find the way; out of sight; unsaved or no longer possessed 迷路的；遺失的 • We were lost for two hours until we finally found her home!
	loss (n.) the act of losing; decrease in value, amount or magnitude 損失 • They sold their house at a great loss because they were in a hurry to sell and move.

passed or **past?**	**passed** (v., past tense of *pass*) to go by a place; to not fail a test; to give somebody something 經過；通過；傳遞 • I have passed by here many times, but never knew you lived here! • "I passed my math test," Judi sighed with relief. • "I've already passed you the catsup, why do you keep asking for it?" Kevin snapped.
	past (adj.) ago; time gone by 過去的 • That store has been closed for the past few years. (n.) time gone by; something that has already happened 過往 • "Learn from the past, but do not live there" is good advice.

principal or **principle?**	**principal** (n.) the leader of a school 校長 • The principal should be your "pal." That's a good way to remember how to spell it!
	principle (n.) a rule or idea 準則 • Honesty is an important principle to live by, so others will trust you.
there or **their** or **they're?**	**there** (adv.) at that place 那裡 • Please wait over there for a moment.
	their (pron.) relating to them as possessors 他們的 • Their children are playing with the toys.
	they're (contraction) they are 他們是 • They're going to be moving soon, and we will miss them greatly.
though or **through** or **threw** or **thorough** or **thought?**	**though** (conj.) although, even though 儘管 • He is still going camping even though it is still raining!
	through (prep.) to go in one side and out the other 穿過 • Ouch! I drove that nail through my finger!!
	threw (v., past tense of *throw*) to pass or toss an object 丟 • He threw the ball so hard and it broke Mr. Chen's window!
	thorough (adj.) careful, detailed 徹底的 • "Make a thorough search for the child," the king told his soldiers.
	thought (v., past tense of *think*) to create a mental image or idea 以為，想 • I thought Chinese and Korean were similar, but now I know I was wrong. (n.) the action of process of thinking 想法 • Some people did not like how Dave often spoke his thoughts freely.

very or **vary?**	**very** (adj.) true, actual, real 正好是 • The train station is in the very heart of Taipei. (adv.) truly, exceedingly (Warning: generally avoid the weak adverbs *very* and *really*) 非常 • Taiwan can be very hot in the summer!
	vary (v.) to change or modify 變化 • Vary your sentence lengths and patterns to keep your readers awake!

whose or **who's?**	**whose** (pron.) that which belongs to whom 誰的 • "Whose dirty socks are these?!" Mom shouted.
	who's (contraction) who is 誰是 • Who's coming to dinner?

In addition to words often confused, these <u>place names</u> are often confused. Tell them apart.

除了上述容易混淆的字詞之外，以下這些地名也常讓人搞混，你要能夠區別它們的不同。

Austria or **Australia?**	奧地利 or 澳洲
	• Austria is a small, mountainous German-speaking country in the heart of Europe. English-speaking Australia is below Indonesia, the only country that is also a continent.

Romania or **Armenia?**	羅馬尼亞 or 亞美尼亞
	• Romania is in Eastern Europe, while Armenia is between Turkey and Southern Russia.

Serbia or **Siberia?**	塞爾維亞 or 西伯利亞
	• Serbia is a small country in Southern Europe; Siberia, however, is huge, the Asian part of Russia.

Washington State or **Washington D.C.?**	華盛頓州 or 華盛頓特區
	• Washington State is in the Northwest corner of the U.S.; Seattle is its most famous city. Washington D.C. is the U.S. capital, on the East Coast of America.

2 Essential Prefixes, Stems, and Suffixes to Know
重要的字首、字根和字尾

English, like Chinese, has so many words you cannot know them all. However, English has a number of prefixes, stems, and suffixes that you *can* memorize, and you can often use these to guess a word's meaning. Most of these prefixes, stems, and suffixes come from Greek or Latin. Over the years, many students have come back and told me that learning these helped them when they took tests or read difficult passages.

英文和中文一樣具有豐富的字彙，你無法記得所有的字。然而英文中有很多的字首、字根和字尾是你可以記住的，而且可用來猜測字的意義。大部分的字首、字根和字尾都是來自希臘文或拉丁文。過去幾年來，學生常回來告訴我說學習這些有助於他們考試或閱讀困難的文章。

Note: Saying "not" in Chinese is easy; just use the word *bu*（不）. In English, however, there are MANY ways to say "not": *a, anti, il, im, in, ir, ex,* and *un*.

在中文裡表達 no 只要說「不」就好了。但在英文中，有很多方式可以表示「不」，例如 a, anti, il, im, in, ir, ex 和 un。

a-: not	**amoral** (adj.) without a moral sense 無關道德觀念的 • Amoral people have no sense of right or wrong.
	asymmetrical (adj.) not symmetrical or balanced 不對稱的 • Nobody wanted to buy the asymmetrical house.
	atypical (adj.) not typical 反常的 • Wearing a cowboy hat in Taipei is atypical.
-anim-: spirit	**animated** (adj.) full of life or spirit 有活力的 • The children were animated on Christmas morning.
	animism (n.) a belief in spirits inhabiting nature 泛靈論 • Many people in parts of Africa and Asia practice animism.
	magnanimous (adj.) very kind or generous; big-hearted 慷慨的 • That gift was very magnanimous of you; thanks!

anti-: not	**antidepressant** (n.) medicine to combat depression 抗憂鬱劑 • Many people find antidepressants helpful.
	antifreeze (n.) liquid to keep your car engine from freezing 防凍劑 • Check your car's antifreeze once a year in cold climates.
	antisocial (adj.) unfriendly; not enjoying people 反社會傾向的 • No one liked the antisocial old man.
auto-: self	**autocratic** (adj.) unlimited power; undemocratic 獨裁的 • Autocratic parents do not share power with their children; they just tell them what to do.
	automatic (adj.) working by itself 自動化的 • The automatic coffee maker is wonderful!
	automobile (n.) a car or motor vehicle 汽車 • The automobile changed the modern world forever because people could go about anywhere they wanted.
bi-: two	**bicentennial** (n.; adj.) 200th anniversary or its celebration 二百週年紀念 • The U.S. celebrated its bicentennial in 1976.
	bilingual (adj.) able to speak two languages 雙語的 • Being bilingual is a great skill.
	bipolar (adj.) having two opposing views; having a psychological disorder with big mood swings 兩極化的 • Her bipolar boss could be kind one moment and mean the next.
-bio-: life	**biography** (n.) the life story about a person 自傳 • I enjoyed reading biographies of presidents when I was a child.
	biology (n.) the study of nature and life 生物學 • Biology is a required course in high school.

-carn-: meat	**carnivore** (n.) a meat-eating animal 肉食性動物 • A lion is a famous carnivore.
	reincarnation (n.) the belief that the dead come back as another person or being 輪迴 • Reincarnation is a major belief of Hinduism.
cent-: one hundred	**cent** (n.) a coin representing 1/100 of a dollar 分 • One cent will not buy you much nowadays.
	century (n.) one hundred years 世紀 • The 20th century saw many changes.
	per cent (n., shown as %) one part in a hundred 百分比 • My bank pays 4 per cent interest on savings.
-cide-: death; to kill	**genocide** (n.) the planned killing of an entire race or group of people 大屠殺 • Hitler's killing of the Jews is probably history's most infamous genocide.
	suicide (n.) the act of killing oneself 自殺 • Teen suicide is a growing problem. We need to spread the message: there is always hope!
-circu-: around	**circular** (adj.) of a round shape or circle pattern 圓的 • Mop the floor in a circular pattern to get it all clean.
	circulation (n.) the steady movement of air, blood, money, etc. 循環，流通 • Regular exercise can help your circulation.
	circumference (n.) the distance around a circle 圓周 • Most students learn how to measure the circumference of a circle.

con-/com-: with	**confidence** (n.) acting with faith and strong feeling 信心 • Give your speeches with confidence to impress your listeners.
	compassion (n.) a strong feeling of love and sympathy 同情 • Moved with compassion, Annie cried at the funeral.
contra-: against	**contraceptive** (n.) devices or methods to avoid pregnancy 避孕用具 • Contraceptives are often used to control family sizes.
	contrast (v.; n.) to compare differences; the differences between two or more items 對比 • Can you write an essay to contrast Taipei and Kaohsiung?
-crac-/-crat-: rule; government	**democracy** (n.) the belief that the people have the power 民主 • Greece was the birthplace of democracy.
	bureaucratic (adj.) leadership marked by inflexible rules and regulations 官僚的 • Bureaucratic government regulations can easily stifle freedom and initiative.
de-: down, away from	**depraved** (adj.) corrupt, evil, perverted 頹廢的；邪惡的 • The depraved man was sentenced to jail for his crimes.
	depression (n.) a deep, long-lasting sad feeling; severe economic downturn 意氣消沉；經濟大蕭條 • Sandy's depression lasted about a year, until she got help.
	descend (v.) to go downward 下降 • The cat slowly descended the stairs, looking for the mouse.
deca-: ten	**decade** (n.) a period of ten years 十年 • "I'm one decade old!" the ten-year-old boasted.
	decameter (n.) ten meters 十公尺 • One hundred decameters make one kilometer.

dia-: across	**dialogue** (n.; v.) two or more characters talking 對話 • Adding some dialogue to your writing can make your work more interesting.
	diameter (n.) the distance across a circle 直徑 • The math class had to measure the diameters of circles.
	diametrically opposed (adj.) complete, polar opposite 南轅北轍 • Mao Zedong and Chiang Kai-shek were diametrically opposed during the Chinese Civil War.
-dom-: house, home	**domestic** (adj.) relating to your home or native country 國內的 • Are you more interested in domestic or foreign news?
	domesticated (adj.) tamed; not wild 馴養的 • Domesticated dogs have been "man's best friend" for thousands of years.
-dorm-: to sleep	**dormant** (adj.) sleeping; not active 休眠的 • Most people ignore the dormant volcano because it has been silent for a long time.
	dormitory (n.) a place where college students live 宿舍 • Moving into your dormitory on your first day of college is a moment you will never forget.
du-: two	**dual** (adj.) consisting of two parts 兩個的 • What Americans call a "divided highway" the British call a "dual carriageway."
	duel (n.) a combat between two persons 決鬥 • In history, men often settled their problems with a duel, fighting until one died.
	duet (n.) two people singing together 二重唱 • People joked that Harmony and Melody could sing a beautiful duet at church.

-dur-: to last	**durable** (adj.) long-lasting; strong; reliable 耐用的 • This refrigerator certainly is durable; it has been running for about twenty years!
	duration (n.) the length of time that something exists or lasts 持續期間 • The workers' strike had a duration of two weeks before the police finally crushed it.
	endurance (n.) the ability to withstand pressure and hardship 耐力 • Endurance is an important virtue; it lets you take stress and keep on going.

-equi-: equal	**equal** (adj.) of the same portion or amount 相等的 • The children wanted equal amounts of ice cream, to be fair.
	equilibrium (n.) balance 平衡 • Sometimes you can lose your equilibrium when you stand up too fast.
	equinox (n.) The date in March or September when spring or autumn begins, and days and nights are of equal length across the world. 春分；秋分 • The Spring Equinox is a happy day because winter is over!

ex-: former	**ex-president** (n.) the former president 前總統 • Ex-President Reagan lived to the age of 93.
	ex-spouse (n.) former husband or wife 前夫，前妻 • Though long divorced, he and his ex-spouse kept going to court, thus enriching their lawyers.

ex-: out	**exit** (n.; v.) the way out; to go out or leave 出口；出去 • To visit Sha-lu, take the first Taichung exit on the Sun Yat-sen Freeway.
	exodus (n.) a mass movement of people out from a place; the second book in the Bible 移出；出埃及記 • There was a large exodus of people from China around 1949.
	export (v.; n.) to sell goods abroad; products sold to other countries 輸出；輸出品 • Taiwan exports computer products around the globe.
-fid-: faith	**confidence** (n.) acting with faith and strong feeling 信心 • "Have confidence in yourself," Mom told Jun-ping before his job interview.
	fidelity (n.) the quality of reliability and trust 忠誠 • Fidelity is key in a successful marriage; the husband and wife have to trust each other and be trustworthy.
-folio-: leaves	**defoliant** (n.) a chemical designed to kill leaves and plants 脫葉劑 • The U.S. used a defoliant in Vietnam that caused much harm.
	foliage (n.) leaves 葉 • Parts of the U.S. and Canada are known for beautiful foliage each autumn when the leaves turn color.
	portfolio (n.) a collection of one's work 作品集 • Laura showed her art portfolio when she applied to work at the museum.

-gen-: life; origin	**gene** (n.) part of DNA or RNA that passes on traits to offspring 基因 • You look the way you do, because of the genes your birth parents gave you.
	genesis (n.) the first book of the Bible; the beginning of something 舊約聖經第一本；創世紀，起源 • The book of Genesis records the story of creation and Adam and Eve.
-geo-: earth	**geography** (n.) the study of the earth and its resources 地理 • Knowing geography is a useful skill, so you will know about the world we live in.
	geology (n.) the study of rocks and physical formations 地質學 • Scientists use geology to find deposits of oil and coal.
-graph-: to write	**autobiography** (n.) the story of the author's life 自傳 • Have you ever wanted to write your autobiography?
	autograph (n.) a signature 簽名 • "May I have your autograph?" the boy asked the famous baseball player.
	graphology (n.) the study of handwriting 筆跡學 • Police and psychologists sometimes use graphology to find criminals or understand how they think.
hemi-: half	**hemisphere** (n.) half of the world, or brain 地球半球；大腦半球 • Your brain has two hemispheres: the right and left.
-herb-: plant	**herbicide** (n.) a chemical to kill plants 除草劑 • Farmers use herbicides to kill weeds, but they may kill butterflies and birds too.
	herbivore (n.) a plant-eating animal 草食性動物 • Elephants, though large, are herbivores.

il-: not	**illegal** (adj.) against the law 違法的 • Murder is illegal everywhere.
	illiterate (adj.) having little education; unable to read or write 未受教育的 • Being illiterate will usually keep you from good jobs.
	illogical (adj.) not logical; senseless 不合邏輯的 • Sam says, "Never go to hospitals, because people die there," but that is an illogical argument.

in-/im-: inside	**introspection** (n.) deep thoughts and reflections about yourself and your life 內省 • In today's busy world, we have to fight to get a few quiet moments for introspection, to think about life.
	introvert (n.) a shy person who gets energy by being alone 內向的人 • The introvert was not unfriendly; she just enjoyed being quiet and listening to others speak.
	import (v,; n.) to bring in goods from abroad; goods brought into a country 進口；進口貨 • The U.S imports more than it exports.

in-/im-: not	**inactive** (adj.) not active; still or dormant 不積極的 • Mom had a hard time waking her inactive teenagers during the summer; they often slept until noon!
	insomnia (n.) the physical condition where one cannot easily sleep 失眠 • Exercising and avoiding caffeine at night can help cure insomnia.
	impractical (adj.) not practical or simple 不實際的 • The harp is a beautiful instrument, but it is impractical; it is hard to move around.

ir-: not	**irregular** (adj.) not regular or normal; unusual 不規律的 • The doctor told him to stop playing tennis for a while because of his irregular heartbeat.
	irresponsible (adj.) not responsible or accountable to another power 不負責的 • "When you stop being so irresponsible, I'll let you go out with your friends again," Mom said.
	irreverent (adj.) not showing proper respect or seriousness 不尊重的 • Most people think laughing at a funeral would be very irreverent.
kilo-: thousand	**kilogram** (n.) a unit of weight, 1,000 grams 公斤 • A kilogram is about two pounds.
	kilometer (n.) a unit of distance, 1,000 meters 公里 • Walking a kilometer or two a day is healthy.
-lib-: free	**liberal** (n.; adj.) a person who is liberal; generous, broad-minded 心胸開闊者；心胸開闊的，開明的 • In theory, a liberal is open to new ideas.
	liberate (v.) to free 解放 • When WW II ended, China was liberated from Japanese control.
	liberty (n.) freedom; the power of choice 自由 • "Give me liberty or give me death," the famous Patrick Henry said, declaring American freedom from England.
-lumin-: to make light; to explain	**illuminate** (v.) to shine light upon; to explain 照亮；啓發 • The speaker illuminated the crowd with her clear, inspirational speech.
	luminous (adj.) giving a small, glowing light 發光的 • The small candles cast a yellow, luminous glow on the walkway as the guests came in.

-magn-: great	**magnificent** (adj.) wonderful, fabulous 華麗的 • "Those floors look magnificent after you waxed them!" Jenny told her husband.
	magnify (v.) to enlarge or make objects look bigger 擴大 • A microscope can easily magnify objects.
mal-: bad; away	**maladjusted** (adj.) not well adjusted 失調的，不適應環境的 • Sadly, many maladjusted children grow up to become criminals.
	malfunction (n.; v.) a breakdown or failure to work properly; to not work properly 損壞 • Argh, this computer malfunction is getting on my nerves!
	malnutrition (n.) lack of proper nutrition 營養失調 • Tragically, while so many people are overweight, millions more are dying from malnutrition.
mater-: mother	**maternal** (adj.) relating to mother or motherhood 母性的 • You can see a bird's natural maternal instinct when she works hard to get food for her chicks.
	matriarch (n.) a woman who rules a family or group 女統治者 • "Mom is truly the matriarch of our family," Dad agreed.
-meter-: to measure	**pedometer** (n.) a device used to measure how many steps one takes 計步器 • We got free pedometers at the health fair, to help us see how far we walk each day.
	speedometer (n.) a device used to measure one's speed 測速計 • "Watch the speedometer," Dad barked at his son who was just learning to drive.

| **mil-/milli-:** one thousand; one thousandth | **millennium** (n.) one-thousand years 千禧年
• When we went from 1999 to the year 2000, the world welcomed a new millennium! |
| | **millimeter** (n.) one-thousandth of a meter 公釐
• Jewelers deal with lengths of mere millimeters. |

mis-: away	**mislead** (v.) to misdirect someone or something 誤導 • We should be honest rather than try to mislead people.
	misplace (v.) to lose or put in the wrong place 誤放 • "I've misplaced my glasses," Miss Petty complained, only to find them on her head!
	mistake (n.; v.) an error; to make an error or flaw 錯誤；犯錯 • We should never be afraid to admit our mistakes; others will respect us for our honesty.

mono-: one	**monotheism** (n.) the belief in one God 一神論 • Judaism, Christianity, and Islam all share a belief in monotheism.
	monotone (n.) a boring voice with one tone and no inflection 單調 • Monotone teachers easily put their students to sleep.
	monotonous (adj.) boring or dull 單調的；無聊的 • Many people find school monotonous.

-nov-: new	**innovation** (n.) a new invention or breakthrough 創新 • Space travel was a great innovation of the 1960s.
	novel (adj.; n.) new; a lengthy book 新的；小說 • The Internet, a novel idea in the 1990s, is now a part of our daily lives.
	novice (n.) a beginner 新手 • Though just a novice, Joanne is already good at the piano.

oct-: eight	**octagon** (n.) an eight-sided figure 八邊形 • The most famous octagon is probably the stop sign.
	octopus (n.) an eight-legged sea creature 章魚 • Though seldom eaten in the West, octopus is popular in Chinese cuisine.
	octogenarian (n.) someone in his or her eighties 80 到 89 歲的人 • Mr. Cross is one of the healthiest octogenarians I know.
pater-: father	**paternalistic** (adj.) heavy-handed, controlling, disrespectful 專制主義的 • The high school students did not like how their teacher treated them like little children; they thought his approach was very paternalistic.
	patriarch (n.) a man who rules a family or group 元老，創始人 • Abraham was a famous patriarch of the Bible; he became father to the Jews and Arabs.
penta-: five	**pentagon** (n.) a five-sided shape 五邊形；美國國防部（五角大廈） • The Pentagon, which houses the U.S. Defense Department, is massive.
-pli-/-ply: to bend	**compliant** (adj.) cooperative, flexible 順從的 • Of the four children, all agree Wendy is the most compliant, because she is always quickest to obey Mom and Dad.
	pliable (adj.) capable of being bent 易曲折的 • Whenever Ya-fan wanted something, she asked her Dad, because he was more pliable than her Mom.
	comply (v.) to obey 順從 • "You have thirty days to comply and pay the fine, or you will go to jail," the judge told the criminal.

-ped-/-pod-: foot	**millipede** (n.) a multi-legged insect 節肢動物 • The millipede has a fitting name: he has lots of legs! **podiatrist** (n.) a doctor specializing in foot care 足科醫生 • Mom made an appointment with a podiatrist when she started having sharp foot pains. **tripod** (n.) a three-legged instrument for holding a camera, etc. 三腳架 • "Everyone stand still while I put the camera on the tripod, then everyone smile and say 'Cheese!'" Dad commanded.
poly-: many	**polygamy** (n.) the practice of having more than one spouse at a time 一夫多妻制；一妻多夫制 • Polygamy is widely practiced in some parts of the Middle East, where a man may have up to four wives at once. **polytheism** (n.) a belief in more than one god 多神教 • The ancient Greeks and Romans believed in polytheism; they had multiple gods and goddesses.
-port-: to carry	**portable** (adj.) capable of being carried 攜帶式的 • Long-ting was so proud on his 10th birthday, when his parents gave him a portable radio. **transport** (v.) to carry or move an item from one place to another 運送，運輸 • Taiwan's export-driven economy requires massive fleets of ships to transport its goods to markets worldwide.
quadr-: four	**quadrant** (n.) a fourth of a circle or another area 四分之一圓 • Berlin was divided into four quadrants after WW II: the Russian, American, British, and French zones. **quadruplets** (n.) four babies born at once to the same mother 四胞胎 • Imagine how busy a home with quadruplets would be!

quart-: one-fourth	**quart** (n.) one-fourth of a gallon 夸脫（約一加侖） • One quart is about one liter. • My growing nephew can drink a quart of milk in one sitting.
	quarter (n.) 25% of something; 25 cents; a specific area 四分之一；25分的硬幣；區 • We will leave in a quarter of an hour: in about 15 minutes. • The old French Quarter is the most famous part of New Orleans.
	quartet (n.) four people singing or playing music together 四重奏 • The string quartet was comprised of two violins, a cello, and a bass.
re-: again	**rebirth** (n.) a new start in life; can be spiritual, physical, cultural, or economic 重生 • Christians believe Jesus gives them a spiritual rebirth. • China has experienced an economic rebirth since the 1980s.
	recycle (v.) to reuse resources so as to reduce waste 回收 • The three R's of environmental protection are Reduce, Reuse, and Recycle.
	reforestation (n.) the act of renewing a forest by planting young trees 重新造林 • Reforestation efforts are helping the environment in many areas.
-reg-: ruler; to rule	**regular** (adj.) normal or usual; on a normal schedule 規律的；正常的 • Regular exercise can help keep you healthy because it is a normal part of your daily routine.
	regulate (v.) to control or manage 管理 • Without stop lights to regulate the traffic, imagine how crazy our roads would be!
	regulation (n.) rules and guidelines to follow 法律規章 • Each school or job has its own set of regulations; follow them to fit in well and succeed.

sept-: seven	**septuplets** (n.) seven children born at once to one mother 七胞胎 • Septuplets are rare, but there are a few!
sol-: only, singular	**solitaire** (n.) a card game played by one person 單人撲克牌遊戲 • Solitaire is a popular card game on the computer.
	solitude (n.) a state of quietness and aloneness 孤獨 • With all the noise and demands of daily life, moments of solitude are a rare and precious gift.
	solo (n.; adj.; adv.) a song performed by one singer or musician; without a companion 獨唱 • The beautiful solo at the Christmas Eve service touched everyone. • After her divorce, Karen had to learn to live solo again.
-spec-: to see, watch	**introspective** (adj.) characterized by looking inward to oneself 內省的 • After several months of introspective contemplation, the couple decided to leave their busy, successful careers in the city and become organic farmers.
	spectator (n.) those who watch an event 旁觀者 • President Reagan once said, "Democracy is not a spectator sport." We all need to get involved.
	spectrum (n.) a wide array or range 範圍；光譜 • One can remember the seven colors of the rainbow spectrum by remembering this name: ROY G. BIV (for red, orange, yellow, green, blue, indigo, and violet).
-theo-: God; religion	**enthusiasm** (n.) a spirit of excitement and purpose 熱忱 • The famous writer Emerson said, "Nothing great was ever accomplished without enthusiasm."
	theocracy (n.) a religious government 神權政治 • Iran has had a theocracy since 1979; Muslim leaders rule the land.
	theology (n.) the study of God and religion 神學 • Many were surprised when the successful businessman quit his job and went to study theology.

-thermo-: heat	**thermal** (adj.; n.) relating to hot water or air; a rising body of hot air 熱的；上升熱氣 • There are some wonderful thermal springs near Taitung and Hualien that are great for relaxing!
	thermometer (n.) a device used to measure temperature 溫度計 • Do you have a thermometer at home?
tri-: three	**tricycle** (n.) a three-wheeled vehicle 三輪車 • Most small kids love riding a tricycle—they enjoy going fast!
	trio (n.) a group of three singers or musicians 三重唱 • The trio helped pay their way through college by giving concerts on weekends.
	triplets (n.) three children born at once to one mother 三胞胎 • Triplets are much rarer than twins.
un-: not	**unruly** (adj.) not easily ruled; wild and out of control 難駕馭的；不守規矩的 • Few people want to be teachers nowadays because of the many unruly students.
	unsaid (adj.) not said or spoken aloud 未說出口的 • Some things are better left unsaid.
uni-: one	**unicycle** (n.) a kind of vehicle with one wheel 單輪腳踏車 • Riding a unicycle required incredible balance and skill.
	unique (adj.) one of a kind; unduplicated 特別的，獨一無二的 • Your fingerprints are unique, because you are unique!

-vert-: to turn	**convert** (v.; n.) to bring over to a belief or view; to change the physical properties of something; one who is converted 使皈依；轉變；改變信仰者 • The missionary tried to persuade his friends to convert to Christianity. • When you travel, you may need to take a converter to convert the electricity from one type of current to another.
	extrovert (n.) one who is outgoing and gets energy from being with people 外向的人 • The popular extrovert was called "the life of the party" because of her enthusiasm and joy of life.
-voc-: to speak, call	**equivocal** (adj.) an unclear message, usually designed to mislead, that can be interpreted in two different ways 模稜兩可的 • Politicians are famous for their equivocal comments designed to try to please everybody.
	vocal (adj.) pertaining to the voice; very loud and outspoken 聲音的；暢所欲言的 • She had eight years of vocal lessons. • The newspaper has been a vocal critic of the mayor for many years, for it often presents unflattering news about her.
	vocation (n.) a strong call to an action; one's job or occupation 使命；職業 (This word, from the 1400s, comes from the belief that God calls one to a particular career or work.) • Despite the low pay, Kay feels a strong calling that teaching is her life's vocation and mission.
-vol-: will; choice	**volition** (n.) the power of choosing; will 選擇；意志 • You should choose your career based on your own volition, not just to please or impress your parents or anyone else.
	volunteer (v.; n.; adj.) to do a job willingly, without pay; one who works willingly, without pay; work done for free 志工 • My parents volunteer to deliver free lunches to senior citizens, so the elderly can stay in their own homes.

3 Additional Resources
附加的學習資源

These are excellent resources to help you as you grow as a writer and several of these authors' ideas are embedded in this book.

以下是很棒的參考書目，可以增進你的寫作能力，其中很多作者的見解已整合至本書中。

- Behrman, Carol H. *Writing Skills Problem Solver*. San Francisco, CA: Jossey-Bass, 2000.

- Bromberg, Murray and Liebb, Julius. *601 Words You Need to Know to Pass Your Exam*. Hauppauge, NY: Barron's, 2005.

- Clark, Roy Peter. *Free to Write: A Journalist Teaches Young Writers*. Portsmouth, NH: Heinemann Educational Books, 1987.

- Flesch, Rudolf. *The Art of Readable Writing*. New York, NY: Macmillan, 1949.

- McWhorter, Katherine T. *Successful College Writing*. New York: Bedford/St. Martin's, 2000.

- Murphy, Raymond. *Grammar in Use: A Self-Study Reference and Practice for Intermediate Students of English (3rd edition)*. Cambridge: Cambridge University Press, 2004.

In addition, below are some outstanding online writing resources.

此外，以下是一些相當實用的線上寫作資源。

- The Purdue Online Writing Lab
普渡大學線上寫作實驗室
(Many consider this one of the finest available.)
http://owl.english.purdue.edu

- Dartmouth Writing Program
  達特茅斯學院寫作計畫
  http://www.dartmouth.edu/~writing/materials/about.shtml

- MIT Online Writing and Communication Center
  麻省理工學院線上寫作和溝通中心
  http://web.mit.edu/writing

- University of North Carolina: The Writing Center
  北卡羅來納大學：寫作中心
  http://www.unc.edu/depts/wcweb

- The Writing Center @ The University of Wisconsin—Madison
  威斯康辛大學麥迪遜分校寫作中心
  http://www.wisc.edu/writing/Handbook/index.html

Final Thoughts
卷後語

Thank you, gentle reader, for joining me on this journey. I hope it has been a fruitful experience, one that will help you become a better writer and communicator.

謝謝各位親愛的讀者，與我一起完成這趟旅程。我希望這對你是次收穫良多的經驗，有助你成為更佳的寫作者與溝通者。

Soli Deo Gloria

榮耀惟獨歸於上帝

國家圖書館出版品預行編目資料

美國老師教你寫出好英文 / Scott Dreyer、廖柏森作 . – 初版 . –
　　臺北市：眾文圖書 . 民 97. 09
　　面；公分

ISBN 978-957-532-357-8（平裝）

1. 英語　2. 作文　3. 寫作法

805.17　　　　　　　　　　　　　　　97014671

定價 320 元

美國老師教你寫出好英文

中華民國九十八年八月　初版四刷

作　　者　Scott Dreyer · 廖柏森
譯　　者　廖柏森
主　　編　陳瑠琍
編　　輯　黃炯睿
美術設計　嚴國綸
發 行 人　黃建和
發 行 所　眾文圖書股份有限公司
　　　　　台北市重慶南路一段 9 號
電　　話　(02) 2311-8168
傳　　真　(02) 2311-9683
劃撥帳號　01048805

局版台業字第 1593 號　　　　　　　　　　　　版權所有 · 請勿翻印

本書若有缺頁、破損或裝訂錯誤，請寄回下列地址更換。
台北縣 231 新店市寶橋路 235 巷 6 弄 2 號 4 樓